DUTY

To Suzenne
Best Wishes

JEFF STEPHENSON

J Stephenson

Published by Write on the Tyne

First published in Great Britain in 2023 by Write on the Tyne CIC.

This publication is based on true events. It reflects the authors recollections of experiences over time.

Printed and bound in Great Britain by Clays Ltd, Elcograf S.p.A.

ISBN: 978-1-7394882-2-2 (Paperback)

Cover design: Write on the Tyne
Cover image: iStock Photo
Cover model: Jake Stephenson

Published by Write on the Tyne
www.writeonthetyne.com

This is my story, it's the only one I have to tell.

Dedicated to my mam, Harriet Stephenson.

CHAPTER 1
A SHIELDS LAD

My story began on 5th February 1964 when I was born in a town called North Shields, situated on the North East coast of England. North Shields is in the borough of North Tyneside, on the north side of the River Tyne, which separates the city of Newcastle and the borough of Gateshead. We are referred to as "Geordies" in this part of the world and are well known for our friendly personalities and great banter.

You may have heard of the TV personalities Ant and Dec, or the singer Sting — all are from Newcastle. Stan Laurel, of Laurel and Hardy fame, also spent some of his young life living in my town. However, I'm a lot younger, so I didn't get the chance to kick a ball about with Stan before he set off for Hollywood!

Perhaps you know of The Great North Run which takes place in our lovely part of the world each year, attracting runners from across the globe, many raising money for charities. We're celebrated for our stunning city, vast countryside, and award-winning coastline, as well as a few local consumables like Newcastle Brown Ale and pease pudding. And for me, the "Toon," as it's affectionately known, is home. Always has been and likely always will be. I've been away from Newcastle, sometimes for long periods with my career, but I've continuously returned to the place that feels like no other.

Life as Jeffrey George Stephenson began with my mam, Harriet, bringing me into the world at Frater Maternity Home, North Shields in 1964. Within minutes of my arrival, Mam's sister, Violet, was giving birth to my cousin, Carol.

We lived in an area called the Meadow Well, or as we referred to it, "The Ridges." It was a housing estate, heavily dominated by council housing, that became famous for all the wrong reasons in the 1990s. But when I was a kid, living there with my family, it was home and the area had a real sense of community that's still carried in the air today, along with the cold North East breeze.

Mam met my dad, Norman, whilst they were working together in a local factory. Romance gave their shifts extra appeal, and they soon were engaged, then married, before they started our family. I'm one of four children. Norman is the oldest, at 61 years old. I was born next, and I'm now 59 years old, followed by my youngest brother, Andrew who is 57 years old. Lastly, there is our Julie. The only girl, who is 52 years old.

We grew up close as siblings and our bond remains - seeing each other regularly and keeping in touch, despite life's demands. We had a good upbringing with Mam and Dad working hard to provide for us. There were always challenges in those days, same as we have today just in different ways, but my childhood was happy, full of adventure, and positive memories.

I don't have memories of my grandparents as both sets died when I was younger. However, I had many aunts and uncles, and plenty of cousins. Back then, families were big like in the 1970s TV show, *The Waltons*. Auntie Violet, Mam's sister, lived nearby and in my early years, we would play on the streets with our cousins, kicking a ball for hours on end until the sun went down.

Mam was a traditional housewife, looking after us kids and keeping the home until we were older, whilst Dad worked as a fitter/turner in Hall Sections, a local factory. Growing up, Dad was made redundant from Hall Sections and began working at the docks. The early 1960s were a time of growth and prosperity in our area. Recovery and development of industry after the end of the Second World War meant Swan Hunter, in Wallsend, and Smith's Dock, in North Shields, were producing and repairing ships. The Ministry was built and provided office jobs in the civil service for thousands of people from the area. However, things changed as the late 1960s approached, with coal mines closing in neighbouring villages across Northumberland, Tyne and Wear, and Durham.

Dad always worked hard, as most men did in those days — long hours and heavy work. He instilled a strong work ethic in all of us that I still carry today and have passed on to my own children. The life lessons informally taught that are shared between generations.

Home in the Meadow Well was crowded, with the six of us living in a three-bedroomed house. Luckily for Julie, this meant she had her own bedroom, whilst me and my two brothers were squashed into a room together. It was carnage and never quiet but there were more laughs than arguments.

We were the best of friends (most of the time) in our younger days, then as we got a little older, personalities started to develop alongside new friendships with neighbourhood kids and friends from school. It was an open house around the estate, with front doors never closed. Big families, crazy in a lot of ways, but the salt of the earth. Of course, there were some homes you would avoid, with varying degrees of characters.

Us kids would all pile into each other's homes, and there was always someone to play with. A close-knit community where my mates on the estate were looked after by my parents, just as I was by theirs. A community of carers. Everyone was welcome in each other's homes and if we needed anything, there was a never-ending stream of offers, kindness, and smiles — values that were always in fashion.

We grew up playing around the doors in the fresh air, running around until we were exhausted. Even in the cold North East of England, we didn't often feel the chill; we just wanted to be out with our mates. It never seemed boring or unsafe. At weekends and during school holidays, we would rush out to play, only interrupted by Mam's voice shouting to us from the front door, telling us it was teatime. Ravenous from all the running about but scared we would miss out on playing, we would listen to our stomachs and return indoors for our fill and hoping we could perhaps play out again after mealtime.

Groups of us played around the estate, gathering to play street games like tin-o-block. This would involve an old tin and two gangs. It sounds like a simple game, and it was — something that cost nothing but brought hours of fun and teamwork. Two teams would be decided, and a tin would be kicked by a member of one gang. The other team would run off hiding. The tin-kicking gang had to find the others and bring them back to the tin. The trick was if one of your team that was hiding from the tin-kicking team managed to get back to the tin unfound, they could kick the tin and those who had been found could run off again. Hours and hours of laughs.

We used our imagination a lot in those days, even with an empty tin of beans! Our other love was footy. We were all football mad, and it was a big part of my life both in and out of school. Anywhere we could kick a ball, we would be there.

I grew up in an era of what felt like care-free innocence. Kids were still kids — picking on each other, arguing, and joking, but it always felt like sharing a chocolate bar afterwards made everything in the world okay. A good game of football could solve any disagreement, if not solve it, it would definitely divert a disagreement to another one about who was off-side or a brutal tackle. They were happy days when life felt like a daily adventure and, in some ways, we all slept better at night, adults and kids.

Traditions were important when I was growing up. There were routines and expectations that families and communities held. Sundays were a day of rest and shops weren't open. It was time for family, cooking, cleaning, relaxation, and also church for many. We weren't a religion-practising family so for us, the day was all about winding up the week and getting ready for the week ahead. Sunday was also bath day, and we would take turns getting a good wash before school the next day.

I remember on Sunday mornings, Mam used to prepare the Sunday roast with the radio playing. She would hum along as music filled the house, Slim Whitman blasting out as Mam peeled and chopped vegetables and got the meat ready for our favourite meal of the week. Never a rush, just enjoying the process and producing delicious food that we all ate together.

I've always been a fussy eater, but Mam was a great cook. We would have homemade stodgy meals like mince and dumplings, pies, stews, and heaps of vegetables. I didn't like most vegetables, so it was potatoes for me. Mam's food was good, unlike the muck I had to eat at school. She would make puddings from scratch, and we'd tuck into crumbles with custard or rice pudding made with love. All of us, around the table to eat as a family. Another tradition that we wouldn't dare deviate from but something we all enjoyed and despite thinking about playing out after most meals, we never did on a Sunday.

Dad worked Monday-Friday so on a Sunday he was able to have tea with us as a family. He'd normally have a nap after tea then go to the club to share a few pints with friends. Dad was a good father, but like most men of that era, he didn't show a lot of emotion. It was how men were in the 1960s and 1970s and still are to some degree today, however, we knew we were cared for and loved. Mam was more affectionate but there was a lot of us to dish the love out to. Actions always meant more than words to us, and they still do for me now, as an adult and a father myself.

In the summer holidays, we would go away as a family. Coach trips for the odd day out here and there, or weeks away to Filey and holidays to Butlins. My parents booked trips through the local coach company, Priory Travel, and it would be something for us all to look forward to as we counted down the days left at school.

The summer holidays were amazing, and the days felt endless — as if time had been paused — allowing us to enjoy being kids without the cloud of adult responsibilities. Playing out all day in the sun and being allowed to stay out late at night, before it eventually got dark, despite our energy still glowing. We would build go-carts out of any items we could find; anything we could use we utilised to build our winning vehicle.

As we grew older, we would wander out of the streets to nearby places. It felt like the other side of the world as we walked for what we thought was miles and miles on an epic exploration — in reality, it was only a mile or so away. A big adventure, hanging around the old, disused rail lines, climbing trees, and kicking a ball about in a park. Never seeing any danger, just fun. Boundless summer days, until it was September and back to the mundanity of the next school year.

Christmas was also a time for family. We would do what all kids do on Christmas Eve and refuse to sleep. I remember sitting on the stairs on Christmas Eve, not wanting to go to bed; my parents unable to put the presents out. Only for them to be woken up a few hours later by our enthusiastic clapping at daft o'clock and screaming it was Christmas at ear-piercing levels, desperate to see what Santa had left for us! We would pester Mam and Dad to get up in the pitch black of the winter morning and they would eventually give in, dragging themselves out of slumber to placate the four children who were crawling up the wall with excited energy and anticipation.

The lounge carpet would be covered with four piles of presents. It would feel like the best day of our young lives. Big smiles and eyes wide, seeing all the shiny wrapping paper, neatly and lovingly covering our gifts that we were eager to open, ripping them apart like two dogs fighting over a scrap of meat. As we grew up, the piles became smaller as the presents became more expensive, and the desirable gifts became things like Chopper bikes.

Christmas Day was a time when all the kids from the estate would be out navigating their new, sparkling bikes through the streets. Seeing who had got which bike and wondering who could do the best tricks or go the fastest. We would build ramps and go speeding up to them, shooting off with no fear of falling. Great memories of childhood that still feel like yesterday.

CHAPTER 2
SCHOOL DINNERS
AND FOOTBALL DREAMS

Much of school also still feels like yesterday, some of it for the wrong reasons. On the whole, school was average for me. I didn't hate it, but I certainly didn't love it. I tried my best and had great friends, but I was never massively interested in learning; I was more interested in the sport and social side than the academic education.

My brothers and me were all into sports and played on the school football teams. It meant more time with my classmates doing something that I was good at and that excited me way more than maths or science ever did. I attended the same school as my brothers or "wor kid," as we refer to our siblings in our part of the world.

Our school, Queen Victoria School, was a local state school that was old-fashioned with an institutional feel. One of the absolute worst things about school for me was the disgusting school dinners. They were a vile daily serving of lumpy mashed potato, tasteless vegetables, and rubbery meat that would likely bounce higher than a tennis ball if dropped to the floor. The impending doom of having to face them made me feel nauseous all morning. The meals always seemed to come soaked in gravy, or some unidentifiable sauce, that was thinner than water with clots of congealed gunk sporadically floating around in it. I'm sure they scooped it out of the local stream!

Well before the times of Jamie Oliver's school meals campaign, everything seemed to bleed into whatever it shared a plate with. Bean juice would soak into fish which merged into potato. As a fussy eater, it was hell, and I would borderline beg for certain things not to be placed on my plate or my bowl only for my polite request to be ignored and my meat or pudding to be drenched in a liquid that made me want to vomit.

I remember one time in the canteen when a dinner lady came up behind me where I was sitting, desperately trying to avoid the runny, beige, unappealing food that seemed to travel by itself around my plate. I jumped slightly in my seat as she took hold of my arms and began cutting up the meal on my plate.

'Come on, Jeffrey, get it eaten up,' she said sternly, as I looked, eyes wide at the plate of supposed cauliflower and mash, then at her as she stood, her hands now on her hips, glaring down at me.

I'll never forget the absolute sickness I felt, and I still can't eat cauliflower to this day. School meals scarred me for life. Discipline at school, and out of school, was vastly different when I was a youngster, and thankfully some practices no longer happen. Children were voiceless in many ways and the opinions of kids weren't asked for as they were seen as not being important.

Even at an age where kids knew what they wanted and had the autonomy to make decisions, they were still simply kids and adults knew better. There was little room for identity. You had to fit into a box in school, a role and follow opinions and decisions imposed onto you, including eating congealed, colourless gloop that you didn't like!

During my school days, corporal punishment was used in education. This meant that the threat of violence was acceptable as a form of ensuring the "correct" behaviour as a pupil, but it also meant that the use of violence was tolerated if kids misbehaved. I remember one form teacher - an assertive, experienced teacher that I respected. This particular teacher had a slipper that sat menacingly on his desk, dangling slightly over the edge as if it would snap at you like a dog as you passed. It was there as a deterrent, or a weapon to smack us with if we did something wrong; and the teacher wasn't scared to use it.

At that time, we would never have referred to the slipper, or a strap, or a cane, all of which were used to inflict discipline through pain, as weapons. But in reality, that's what they were. It was accepted, normal, not questioned. The threat of the object resulted in respect, most of the time, but that respect was built on a foundation of fear. Some kids naturally received corporal punishment more than others. They were the pupils that perhaps rebelled, wouldn't, or couldn't do as they were told, didn't listen, or talked too much. Kids who didn't do their homework, couldn't get the right answer, had fights, or were consistently late.

These behaviours still happen in schools today, kids are kids, and they are navigating life and adolescence. Learning and growing up; school can be hard for many but there seems to be more exploration into why kids may behave in certain ways now. Kids at my school were quickly labelled as "naughty." There wasn't any consideration or compassion for some children potentially having learning barriers, difficulties, or disabilities; children who might be living in broken families, in poverty, being abused, dealing with mental illness, and so much more.

It was basically the attitude that if you didn't conform and follow the rules, you were punished. Simple as that. If "bad" behaviour continued, you would be sent to the headmaster who had a thick strap of leather, and he would repeatedly smack your hands with it. This made me conform most of the time, as I didn't want to be belted, caned, or whacked with a size 9 firm slipper that taunted me in the classroom each day. But I was still a kid and was learning about myself and the world around me.

As a child, you didn't analyse those scenarios and behaviours, because they were the norm. But it's hard to imagine teachers physically assaulting children in schools nowadays. Corporal punishment was banned in state schools in England in 1987 but it was not abolished in private schools until 1999.*

I'm sure that there would have been many kids over the time of corporal punishment, that were traumatised by what they experienced. For some, perhaps school was the only discipline they experienced. For many, I'm sure fear was the catalyst to respecting rules and boundaries. Respect and fear — there's a fine line between them. But for us, as kids at school, it was normal, and we got on with it. I learnt a level of discipline at school and went on to use this in my career in some ways.

My favourite lesson throughout school was Physical Education (P.E.). Any sports that I could get involved in, I did. I participated in all those on offer and I was on the teams for various sports. Being full of energy and playing sports on breaks, then not eating the school dinners meant that there was very little meat on my skinny frame. It was a good job Mam was a good cook and I got my fill at home to keep me going.

At school, I had plenty of friends and I fitted in with, which undoubtedly made my educational experience more pleasant. Some of the friendships made throughout my education still exist now. Many of these mates I had even before school because we knew each other from the estate. Lifelong pals.

* Reference: www.localhistories.org

There were a few schools in the area but in the Meadow Well, most of the kids went to Queen Victoria School, and St Cuthbert's School over the road. The rivalry between the schools was serious. I remember one year; it was a bitter winter and snow covered the streets. Being kids, we hardly felt the cold. Instead, we wanted to be out playing in the glistening, inviting white mass that covered the ground, eager to mess about and pelt snowballs at one another. But why throw them at each other when we could fling them at the kids from St. Cuthbert's, as it was opposite our school? A brilliant memory I have is of us all launching snowballs at the St. Cuthbert's enemy kids, full force, then ducking to avoid the incoming attack.

At the age of 11 we all moved to the same senior school, friends staying together. Senior school meant changes around education but also the introduction of new people, away from the primary school that had become our comfort blanket. My senior school was called Ralph Gardner School and there was something akin to a Mexican stand-off, with the new kids from different estates and parts of the town as they were introduced to already established friendship groups.

On top of this, we all had to adjust to changes in routines, new teachers, and new expectations. Students were placed in bands in class, indicating our level of capability in certain subjects. Determined by exams, we were moved into the band that was pitched at our learning level. Everyone dreaded being put in the bottom band where people would think you were thick as mince and wouldn't achieve anything. Of course, it wasn't true, but for us kids, it was something no one wanted, and it had a stigma attached to it. Luckily, I was placed in the middle sets with some of my mates.

Discipline and deterrents from misbehaving were slightly different at senior school and now included detention and extra homework. There were still physical punishments such as the odd teacher clipping you over the head if you were late or forgot something. No questioning the kids as to why, just an immediate clunk on the head by the teacher's knuckles or similar. Teachers would be memorable for either frightening us or inspiring us. The one's in between were easy to forget.

I do remember one teacher that made an impact on me. It was my music teacher, and it was a lesson I wasn't interested in that always felt like an opportunity to skive. The teacher, Mrs Turnbull, was blind and she was incredible as was her guide dog, who remained by her side in the class. What made her quite exceptional was that she would be playing away on the piano but still knew exactly what was going on in the class. I would be mucking about as she tinkled the piano keys, perhaps I'd be chatting with a mate or messing around and she would shout,

'Stop it, Jeffrey!' or something similar.

I used to wonder how the hell she knew what I was up to. She was astounding, even if I found the subject as appealing as the school dinners.

In senior school, I wasn't massively studious, but I did what I needed to get through. Again, I continued to play in the sports teams, preferring sports and P.E. to academia, focusing on my love of sports and the close friendships I had made and maintained throughout my childhood. After school, we would go to the local boys' club and play sports. It was organised chaos most of the time, but it was good fun. If you were skilled enough, you would get selected to play for their team and participate in tournaments with other local boys' club teams across the area.

I remember a disturbing event that happened at senior school in 1979. We used to have discos every week, which were often the highlight of the week. One time, we were all there enjoying ourselves and there was some urgency, with the teachers suddenly telling us all to get out. We didn't know what was happening but could see a kafuffle going on in the corner. We all headed out as instructed and an ambulance soon arrived. It transpired that one of our peers had died, a young lad who had experienced a heart attack. We were only around 14 years old. It was the first experience I remember of someone dying —and for a person to die so young, just a kid, one of us with his whole life ahead of him. We were all in shock for a long time.

Another time I remember a lad running riot on the school roof in protest of something or other. He was scaling the building most of the day, shouting and screaming. As kids, we thought it was brilliant and were laughing, whooping, and cheering him in to encourage his rebellion. I didn't have a clue what he was protesting about — perhaps it was the shit school dinners, and I should have joined him! Eventually, the fire service came and got him down with a ladder after giving us some good entertainment and distractions from class.

I tried at school, but things didn't sink in easily and it was sometimes challenging for me. I've found out as an adult that I have concentration issues, which would never have been picked up in my childhood. But school was a good laugh and overall, I enjoyed it, managing to scrape by. There were remedial classes where students who misbehaved or weren't capable were sent. Students who were seen as a pain in the arse were put into massive classes with loads of students going wild. They got even less of a chance to learn and, looking back, it felt like a way to just contain a problem rather than deal with it. Some of my friends were placed there. However, these particular friends have all done well for themselves, which is great to see and a bit of a two-fingers-up to the system that perhaps had them written off as kids.

As there wasn't a massive difference in the ages of my brothers and me, my older brother, Norman, was there to look out for me during my schooling. And I was there for my younger brother, Andrew. We were all okay and didn't get much hassle, but it was good to know we had each other's backs.

Girls started to become a thing for us lads in senior school and I had the odd girlfriend, most of them just lasting a few days or weeks before moving on to the next crush. It was harmless, adolescent relationships and hopefully I didn't break any hearts.

When it came to thinking about my future, I didn't have a clue what my career goals were as I was progressing through school. Usually, kids ended up following in the footsteps of their parents. There was limited career advice and equally limited options for jobs unless you were willing to go on to further study. There were quite clear gendered employment roles, so I would never have thought about working in an office, for example. The lads were offered apprenticeships in mechanics, construction, heavy industry, and manufacturing. It meant you learnt a trade, got a qualification, and a job for life at the end of it. Many of the lads followed their dads into the same jobs, getting apprenticeships where their fathers worked.

I left school at 16 years old. By this time, Norman was in the Royal Marines, and I had fleeting thoughts about joining the Marines myself. However, I applied for a few apprenticeships locally and was invited to interviews. During this time, Norman came home on leave. Hearing the stories of his job in the Marines was amazing and the appeal increased for me. It certainly sounded like a challenge but something that would provide purpose and a chance to develop skills and see the world.

I asked wor kid if he thought I would be able to do it. I was at a crossroads in my young adult life, so his opinion was important to me. Norman looked at me and smiled, then told me that if he could be a Marine, then so could I and that I should give it a go. I admired what my brother was doing, and now the seed was planted.

A thing that shone in my childhood, and continued since I had left school, was my love of sports, particularly football — which was influential in my life. It was part of my identity and helped build my confidence. Football had been my first introduction to being selected, competing, being rejected, and managing failure. It taught me how to respond to success, work as a team, handle responsibilities, and take risks. It was a lesson about the importance to train, and develop motivation, how to communicate, look out for my team, and know the next move of all involved. There was a camaraderie in football, something that I thrived on — being part of a team. And these were skills that ended up being useful and transferable when I began my career in the Royal Marines.

CHAPTER 3
LOCAL LAD LEAVES FOR LYMPSTONE

The seed that Norman planted about the Royal Marines grew rapidly, like a sunflower in summer. At the age of 16, it felt like the Marines could be my chance to experience life, have an adventure, and travel the world. I saw Norman, happy, tanned, confident, and with money in his pocket. He told me about being in Cyprus on tour, meeting new people, and would come home on leave able to enjoy himself with the money he had earned. What was there not to like?

There wasn't a great deal of military history in my family, although my grandad had served in national service and Dad had also been in the forces for a short time. However, Norman was the main draw and I decided to make some enquiries.

Back then, we had to request more information via newspaper advertisements. I cut out a newspaper enquiry form and completed it, requesting further details. After sending it off, I waited with anticipation for a response. In the meantime, I continued to apply for local jobs. Nothing came up of great appeal - if it had then life may have been different. My parents already had their oldest son away with the Royal Marines so although they were supportive, Mam did ask why I wanted to join.

Employment-wise, the natural progression was to go into an apprenticeship and follow in your father's or your uncle's footsteps. It felt almost forced and I didn't want to settle for a job that wasn't for me, that I would likely be stuck in for decades, feeling unfulfilled with the monotony. I wanted to live, to experience life, and travel outside of my hometown.

The world is a massive place, bigger than North Shields, and I was desperate for a piece of it. Luckily, at the time, there were no major conflicts except for Northern Ireland. This helped my mam feel more at ease with her next baby going away – the knowledge that I would likely not be going straight into war.

Eventually, the letter landed on the doormat, and it felt like Christmas during all those childhood years as I read out my invitation to the career's office in Newcastle. A week or so later, I attended the career's office. Norman had given me an idea of what to expect, but I was still a little apprehensive. At the time, some of my friends also applied but none were successful in getting in.

There were a lot of restrictions in those days and the tests were thorough, as they have to be in the armed forces — you are potentially representing your country in battle; they want the right people. And that's before the brutal training regime they put you through, designed to break you down to a crumbling wreck only to build you up again, stronger. The best of the best.

At the career's office, I had the opportunity to talk to a Royal Marines officer. As soon as I set eyes on the officer, I was impressed. He had a presence of someone in authority; confident and dressed in the uniform of power. I immediately respected him, no doubt this was the reaction he sought. I instantly wanted to be in the Royal Marines more than anything I had ever desired, well perhaps second to my team Newcastle United Football Club winning the premier league!

The officer stood up; his green beret perfectly positioned. A mountain of a man and put his hand out to me, referring to me as Mr Stephenson.

It was the first time I had ever been called Mr Stephenson and I already felt a sense of pride. He asked me the obvious question of why I wanted to join the Royal Marines. Addressing him as sir, I answered that I felt it was the right career for me and that employment options at home didn't excite me. I mentioned Norman and he asked about his unit and experience.

It was then down to the essential criteria to pass before even being considered for an interview. The officer asked my height. At that time there was a minimum height requirement and weight limit. I walked over to a tape measure mounted on a wall, biting my lip. I was only small and still growing and I prayed I wouldn't have to try and stand on my tiptoes. It felt like that situation at the fairground we all experienced when we were younger, getting closer to the sign on the most thrilling of rides that had a big arrow, highlighting the height you had to be in order to get on the ride you were so desperate to try. As well as not being tall, I was about six stone soaking wet. I just about made the 5'6" height minimum.

Breathing a sigh of relief, we sat back down, and I was questioned about my exams. I had achieved all my CSE's so that was another tick; and following this, I was required to complete an in-depth application form before being advised I would hear in due course. As I left, I was more determined than ever to join the Royal Marines, feeling it was my destiny.

Again, I patiently waited for any communication to come through the post. I was just leaving school so it meant I could spend time with my friends and explore potential alternative options in case I didn't make the Marines. My heart wasn't fully in exploring a plan B and each day I would check for post and felt like a deflated balloon as the days passed and no letter came. Until one day an envelope addressed to me arrived, dropping onto the hallway mat like a golden ticket from Willy Wonka himself. And with positive news. It was worth the wait.

The letter informed me I had passed the first part of the assessment and was invited to a formal interview and medical for the next stage in the process. Firstly, I visited my local doctor for a medical certificate. I then met with the Marine's doctor for a full health check and assessment, followed by a gruelling interview. Another eye-opening day that despite being slightly invasive, continued to grow my desire to join.

The waiting game began again until I would be informed if I had passed the medical and the interview. After another few weeks of anticipation, and my hopes building like a Premier League football player's bank account, another letter landed on the doormat. It was around September 1980, and this was it — my future on a sheet of paper in a brown envelope. I ripped it open, palms sweaty, and holding my breath. I WAS IN!

I had passed, being offered a place to train to be a potential Royal Marine. The whole street probably heard me celebrating as I read that my joining date would be 9th February 1981, four days after my 17th birthday.

My letter explained I had to be as fit as possible and they had enclosed a suggested exercise plan. Running, press-ups, and sit-ups were all required and a recommendation to commence the training straight away and keep myself fit and healthy until my start date. Adrenaline rushed through my body like a car in a Formula 1 race; and I immediately went for a run to celebrate. It's bizarre to think I was accepted into the armed forces, with a massive amount of responsibility at just 16 years old, before I was legally allowed to drive and drink in a pub.

Talking of pubs, we did go around the drinking haunts, even though we were underage. There was a great group of us who socialised together. Friends were starting apprenticeships and would ask what I was up to. I would happily reply that I was joining the Marines, like wor kid, Norman. My parents were proud, although Mam was, of course, apprehensive. Perhaps not as much as parents would have been in later years when joining the armed forces almost automatically meant you would be going out to Afghanistan or Iraq.

I was still her bairn and, naturally, there was an anxiety despite her being impressed by my determination and direction. I wasn't joining the Marines with thoughts of going to war, to defend and kill if needed. I was joining the Marines to travel the world and immerse myself in the experience, like Norman was. I wanted to go to Cyprus, Hong Kong, and other exotic destinations just as he had on his rest and recuperation.

In the following months before my joining date, I focused on getting as fit as I possibly could. I was always lean and toned due to playing so many sports at school, but this was another level. I wanted to have unbeatable stamina and strength to be the best I could be. I began running and doing strength cardio and soon saw the rewards of my investment in myself. Of course, I made time to go out with the lads, but I was focused and disciplined — preparation for the strict regime of Royal Marines training. I still couldn't eat anything green, but I managed the odd carrot to try and improve my nutrition. There were limits though!

I turned 17 years old on 5th February 1981 and four short days later, it was time to leave home. It's strange as I look at 17-year-olds these days, who seem older than we were at 17, and it's hard to imagine that I joined the Marines at that same age. We were also in a world without internet and most kids hadn't travelled outside of their local towns or outside of the UK. I had no way of researching places except at the library, which I didn't visit unless I had to.

I was required to attend the Royal Marines base in a smart suit, so my mam took me to get new clothing, then I was all packed and ready to leave. My first time away from home, alone, and although the excitement was pumping through my veins, there was also a glimmer of a frightened child inside me. I said my goodbyes to Mam, Andrew, and Julie, then Dad travelled with me to the train station in Newcastle. As we travelled away from my house, street, estate, and town, I swallowed down the thought that I would miss home and all it stood for. A new adventure awaited, and I knew it would make me a man, in one way or another.

Dad said more to me on the journey up to Newcastle than he had in a long time. It was his moment, his chance to talk to me man-to-man, but still with that ever-protective father role. We said goodbye at the train station. A firm handshake and a smile, as he wished me well. Dad wasn't an emotional man, but I knew he was proud of me. His son taking another step in the world, a step of great independence, and I hoped I could continue to make him proud.

My train was to Lympstone Commando railway station, near Exeter, and as I stepped onto the train, I felt a wave of gratitude that I had a possible dream career ahead of me. A couple of hours later I was less impressed with myself as I sat on the train, my sandwiches long gone, bored and with very little money in my pocket. The train journey to Lympstone Commando took eight hours, which felt like forever when I had little to occupy myself and had no scran left.

However, travelling down the country, glancing out of the window now and then, was lovely; seeing all new places as we sped by. The furthest distance away from home I had been to was Yorkshire on holiday or to away games supporting my beloved football team, Newcastle United. We passed so many new places, most of which I had never heard of. It was an education in itself – people embarking on the train with different accents and different ethnicities. The train eventually arrived in Exeter where I disembarked and got on another train that would take me to Lympstone Commando, the Royal Marines training centre.

I remember looking around for lads who may also be going to Lympstone Commando. Spotting some potential Marine trainees in smart clothes of a similar age to me, I hoped they would be heading my way. The train pulled into the station, and I could see massive walls, climbing frames, and water. I knew I had arrived. As I began to get up from my seat, my legs shaking, reality hit, and I was shitting myself wondering what the hell was going to happen and thinking how far away from home I was.

I slowly got off the train, looking around at some of the other young lads. A drill instructor in full attire, a green beret, and holding a stick greeted us. He looked like someone out of a war film with muscles to match a weightlifter. Sternly and loudly, he told us where to stand. We followed instructions, scurrying clumsily like animals freed from cages. There were six of us and we stood in a line as he ticked off our names, before we adhered to the drill instructor's orders to follow him quickly to our base.

It consisted of grey, dull buildings with no warmth. Glancing across the area, there were troops running or marching everywhere. We were instructed not to look around until we reached a building that would be our dorm. Ordered inside, we had to find a bed space and a locker then wait for further instruction. By this time, around 25 men were already there. Everyone shared a hello and handshake before frantically finding a space to call our bed amongst all the identical metal beds with matching, colourless bedding, and a hessian sack blanket.

There were around 30 beds on each side of the wall and a few windows. I will never forget how spotless the floor was. It was gleaming and could almost be used as a mirror. Alongside the illuminating floor, there were metal bins that didn't have a single mark or smear on them. I remember thinking that keeping the floor and bins pristine must be someone's job and I prayed it wouldn't be mine.

Recruits kept arriving until around midnight and were marched into the dorm like sheep by the same drill instructor. When the last lot arrived, he advised us that it was time to sleep and that we would all be up at 5:30 am to be showered and dressed for breakfast at 6:00 am. There were no pleasantries, instead the message of,

'Make sure you're fucking up, clean, and fucking ready for 6:00 am.'

I lay in bed, exasperated, exhausted, and thinking what the fuck have I got myself into. Welcome to the Royal Marines!

CHAPTER 4
A SHOCK TO THE SYSTEM

I'll use the word sleep loosely for that first night in Lympstone. As well as the kick into the reality of what was to come, I was surrounded by almost 60 lads snoring, farting, sleep-talking, and probably crying. I was in a strange bed with scratchy blankets, in what felt like the start of a possible horror film, absolutely shattered, and with my mind in overdrive as to what may happen next. Even the tales from Norman didn't feel like preparation for the reality. I struggled to get the tiniest amount of sleep on that first night like I imagine so many of the other recruits did. When I eventually fell asleep, I'm certain it was from pure mental and physical exhaustion. Then what felt like ten minutes later, the door burst open with a morning message blasted of,

'160 Troop, get up you fuckers!'

There was me, expecting a cup of coffee and a biscuit with a smile. No chance. Within the dorm of 50-60 lads, we had six showers and four sinks to wash in. There was no organisation and the bigger and older lads got in there to wash first, like bulls stampeding through a field. The showers were freezing, surely the coldest in the world and at 5:30 am, it felt like torture as we all rushed through the morning routine. We were yet to receive uniforms so after our wash in the shower that couldn't possibly get any colder, we had to put our civilian clothes back on, ready to be marched down to breakfast.

The drill sergeant returned and ordered us into three lines. Everywhere we went from then on was in three lines or ranks. We learnt this quickly and would navigate into our line at super speed to get ready for the next instruction barked at us.

There were some "*Dad's Army,*" incidents in those first few days. The drill sergeant would order us to turn left when we were in our ranks, marching like maniacs, and half the unit would turn right, only to get bawled at with lots of expletives. It was hard not to laugh but we were all shit scared of getting a telling off.

That first morning, the drill sergeant ran off screaming at us to follow him and we all went rushing after him like lost sheep. I learnt that day that you ran or marched everywhere, there was never a slow pace and if you forgot once, you would never forget a second time. You were either asleep or moving.

On reaching the canteen, or galley as we call it in the Royal Marines, due to our naval heritage, we were all hurried inside. It was vast and noisy, and as recruits, we were marched to the front. The food was a never-ending display, divine smells tickling our nasal receptors with inviting allure. A colourful presentation of everything and anything you could wish for. Each mealtime was the same stunning food with plenty of choice and as much as you wanted.

However, you had to eat it faster than Usain Bolt can run, not just on this occasion, but every mealtime. It meant food was never enjoyable and I lost count of the number of lads throwing up all over the place in between orders and exercises. I soon learnt to inhale my food and not consume too much in fear of vomiting or having diarrhoea before we would be ordered outside by a booming voice.

The first day involved a lot of paperwork and admission processes. After breakfast, we returned to the block and met our training team. This consisted of four corporals, one sergeant, and a troop officer. We were given a quick talk on do's and don'ts and then instructed to go and get our haircut. I already had a skinhead, but some men had long hair and hairstyles that took a lot of grooming. It all came off and even with my skinhead, the barber still managed to take off a layer of hair. There was no asking this barber for a "George Michael" haircut!

We were all beginning to look similar, something that the Marines wanted – a new identity for each of us but an identity that barely distinguished us from the next person standing to attention by our side. We were now theirs, the property of the Royal Marines, as they slowly stripped us down to the bone to build us back up.

After the scalping, we went to receive our equipment. A massive kit bag was thrown our way followed by us all stepping forward one by one to an officer who asked us our size. Everyone was issued three shirts, three pairs of trousers, or denims as they were called, a pair of boots, shoes, underwear, and socks. All the items had to be put in our kit bag, at speed as the conveyor belt of trainees kept moving and the orders kept being barked.

Next on the agenda was the medical which included completing more forms as well as receiving vaccinations for illnesses such as malaria, in preparation for a time when we would be posted abroad. It was here I hit a hurdle as one of the medications had to be taken in a sugar lump. My peculiar palette stood to attention. I was unable to eat sugar in its raw form and never ate it at home, not even a sprinkling of the sweet crystals on my breakfast cereal. Seeing the sugar lump gave me my own lump in my throat as it tightened with the anxiety that rippled over my body with the dread of having to consume it. I was instructed to take the sugar lump by the doctor, and I advised him I couldn't, stating I would be sick. He looked at me, shaking his head and replied with an abrupt,

'You have to fucking take it.'

There was no negotiation in the Marines, no reasoning. Everything was black or white and at this point, the sugar lump had to be eaten, no excuses, no finding a solution. My heart was racing and the knowledge that all the troops were outside waiting for me did nothing to ease my discomfort. I took a deep breath and stared at this tiny sugar lump that in my eyes, looked as big as a brick. Eventually, after much gagging, I managed to swallow the sugar cube. As I left the office and reunited with the troops outside, I received a massive round of applause and an equally large mocking from the many sets of eyes staring at me followed with,

'Right, you stupid bastard, get in line,' by the corporal. And we were off again, dashing back to the block for the next process, as my cheeks burnt a cherry red.

Returning to the block, the training team showed us how to iron our kit. This wasn't a quick run-over of the iron on your T-shirt ironing lesson. This was more borderline psychopathic iron-your-crease-to-a-specific-length precision ironing session, that felt like an impossible task for someone who always had their mam iron their clothes.

Alongside this was a lesson on how to clean and maintain your clothes, through handwashing and care. The corporal demonstrated, bellowing out the process, and asking us if we understood. Everyone had to answer quickly before the next part of intricate instructions were screamed at us. The corporal would get us all to reply that we had understood before moving on to the next step. This meant that during daily inspections, we couldn't use the excuse that we didn't know how to iron or wash, or whatever the training team were showing us as we'd all stated we understood. It was a pressure cooker of speed, anxiety, and desperate attempts to absorb and retain information.

At the time it was mind-blowing, frightening, and stressful but this attention to detail and building up of each person as part of a machine was about the exactness that in conflict, is essential. Precision that means life or death. Instruction and ability to adhere to orders, conform, and the skill of the most intricate of details was, and is, survival in the military. I knew the importance of this after training, but at the time it felt like a form of mental and physical torture that went on hour after hour, day after day, week after week. No let up, no respite.

We were shown how to clean our boots and our physical training (PT) kit which included trying to keep white plimsolls, that were worn outside, clean. It felt like some insane psychological experiment, all of this on day one after little sleep. Talk about a shock to the system. Eventually, after learning the obsessive detail of cleaning and maintaining our kit, we were rushed down to the galley for our tea. After wolfing it down like starving animals — which I quickly realised was the new way I would be eating each meal — we were dashed back up to the block where the nightmare got a lot worse.

It's still etched in my mind, four decades later. We all entered the dorm, and another corporal was there to show us how to wash ourselves — yes, how to wash our adult bodies! He boldly stripped off and went in the shower, as if returning from a gym session. All of us gathered round to observe him washing every single square inch of his body, with running, abrupt commentary and screaming at us to acknowledge understanding of how to wash our arse.

It would have been a picture to see everyone's face, but of course, you couldn't look away from the naked corporal soaping his bits, because you would receive another form of bollocking – a telling off by one of the other training team members who would be eagle-eyeing you and ensuring you were taking it all in, even the bits that you really wanted to close your eyes to and shut out.

So, there we all were, watching the corporal wash his body parts and telling us how to keep ourselves clean, balls and all. I was one of the youngest, at just turned 17 years old, but there were men a lot older than me who still had to listen to a lecture and watch an explicit demonstration of how to wash.

'Everyone understand how to wash?' he screamed at us all and we all immediately replied,

'Yes, corporal.'

I'll never get that out of my head. Although it sounds like a weird comedy sketch, there was also a lesson in this. Hygiene is essential in the Marines. If you weren't clean, it increased chances of infection which could mean you were out of action and a liability to your troop. Every single bit of skin had to be cleansed, every hair washed. It was beyond methodical, but it worked. I imagine every man who has been in the Marines and other armed forces still has the most rigorous of hygiene routines.

It wasn't the end of the day yet and after the lesson on how to wash our bodies, the next training lesson started. Before we began, I remember that someone had dropped something. One of the corporals screamed at him, ordering him to do 20 press-ups. The corporal glanced at me and for some reason, he thought that I was sniggering. I was likely sniggering out of embarrassment, and he came right up to me, an uncomfortable closeness. This was a bloke who was huge in height, with shoulders that looked as wide as a doorframe. He bent down and came within nose-touching distance, glaring at me, then snarled,

'Right, you Geordie cunt, I'll make sure you don't make it to the end of the week.'

I didn't know what to do as I felt my pulse throbbing in my head. I was battling at that moment with whether to cry or whether to headbutt him. I could feel his hot breath on my face as his mouth twisted in disgust and malice just inches away from mine. I realised if I reacted in either of those ways, I would be out of the Marines. It was a big test for me. No one had ever made me feel so intimidated in a situation where I knew I couldn't respond how I would in the "real world." Swallowing my fear and pride I replied,

'Yes, corporal.' All the while thinking in my head, *I'll fucking show you.*

That was my first day in the Royal Marines. It's a fact that during the first couple of weeks of Royal Marines training, the training team's job is to get rid of the recruits who don't have the strength, stamina, and mental agility to go on. To dispose of the rubbish. They don't want to invest in people who won't make the grade. Those who can't handle it, aren't strong enough and could be a liability out in action, a risk to the whole troop. It's as simple as that.

It felt like bullying, and I'm certain in many cases some of the training team exerted too much power and misused their authority but it was a role they had to play, a job, and they may have gone home to their families a completely different person, perhaps. But almost everything we went through felt like a test and for a purpose, even if we were blind to it at the time.

The Royal Marines training is one of the longest training programmes in the world, at 32 weeks. It's seen as the elite of the armed forces, the best of the best, and that's what they want out of their troops. They want the best to get to the end of the gruelling training, ditching those who don't make the grade on the way, like broken tiles — useless. I'm sure things have changed with regards to the approach in the delivery of the training but no doubt it is still more intense than most people can imagine. They are training killers; it's not going to be crafts and yoga. Machines before humans, there to do a job.

It was the early hours of the morning, and finally time for sleep. I lay in bed wondering what the hell I was doing. This reoccurring thought lasted a few weeks, entering my head more than once as I wondered why I was there and if I could tolerate the training any longer. It would be so easy to leave and return to the comfort of North Shields and the familiar security home provided. I wanted to leave, to quit, on many occasions. However, the determined streak in me wanted to prove myself, not only to show myself and my family I could do it, but also the corporal who told me that he would watch me fail. That bastard kept me going.

Day two started as every day would; awake at 5:30 am, breakfast at 6:00 am, and then straight into the day's brutal regime. We were ordered to wear our PT kit and marched to the gym where we were greeted by the physical training instructors. They were mountains of men, bodies carved in stone, and we were welcomed with a booming,

'Right, you fuckers run to that wall, go! Press-ups, go!'

Followed by instruction after instruction non-stop for an hour and a half. After a physical beasting, we had an afternoon of maths and English testing. The Marines used a testing system called NAMET (Naval Maths and English Tests). I remember I scored just enough to pass, and I was told that if I went for promotion in the future, I would require a better score. Promotion was the absolute last thing on my mind at that time, surviving each hour was my focus.

After inhaling dinner that night, we were shown how to put our kit into our lockers properly. Everything had a place, and it was not to be disrupted or changed in any way. Items of clothing had to be folded into the size of a magazine to go into the locker. Shirts, trousers, gym kit, all ironed and folded. This practice was ingrained in us, and we had to get it perfect for inspections. The habits I learnt in the Marines have never left me. My partner, Gillian, calls them my "Jeff-isms." They never dissolve or disappear, instead, they become part of you, your DNA.

After we were shown how to organise our lockers and everyone stated they understood, locker inspection became a regular thing. Inspections of something or another were a daily test, and we never passed the first time. It was as if passing the first time could make us complacent. An imperfection would always be identified and if it was lockers, they would be turned over by the corporals, completely trashed, and we had to spend the next few hours tidying them in meticulous routine to be re-inspected.

Belongings would be pelted across the dorm, and we would all scurry like rats, salvaging our items to bring back to our locker and try again to meet their standard. It was utterly head-battering, and I was often pulled up about my locker and other things.

I was one of the youngest and had limited life experience, so the presentation tasks were most definitely one of my weaker points. Each of our items had to have our name and service number stencilled in. My name was long, so it took me forever, and alongside our names, we had to stencil in our service number, mine being PO41937Y. This was required on everything you owned whether it be your clothes, toothbrush, mirror, anything – always that number, our branding.

In those first few days, we became familiar with each other's names but there was no chance to talk and get to know each other. The odd conversations whilst we were polishing our boots at midnight maybe, but in these early days, we were getting used to being in each other's space and remembering surnames.

When we eventually got to bed on night two and onwards, sleep wouldn't be forthcoming, despite mental and physical exhaustion. It wasn't like we were snuggling up in our comfy beds at home. This was a room full of other men, in a basic bed. Instead of feelings of cosy contentment, all I could think was what the fuck will we be doing tomorrow? Or what the hell do I need to remember? This went on for weeks, nerves shot. There was no drifting off into elated dreamland. Instead, it felt like the nightmare was only going to become more horrific!

CHAPTER 5
FOG ON THE TYNE

The next day we were ordered out of bed at 5:30 am for day three of our training. An important part of this day was the recruits swearing their oath of allegiance. This involved us all declaring our allegiance, our commitment to Queen and country. All armed forces personnel must do this, and we were taken into a room where a picture of Queen Elizabeth the Second hung on the wall and shown a board with the oath that we had to recite:

'I swear by Almighty God that I will be faithful and bear true allegiance to Her Majesty Queen Elizabeth the Second, Her heirs and successors and that I will, as in duty bound, honestly and faithfully defend Her Majesty, her heirs and successors, in person, crown and dignity against all enemies, and will observe and obey all orders of Her Majesty, her heirs and successors, and of the generals and officers set over me. So help me God.' *

* Reference: Oath of Allegiance (United Kingdom) - Armed Forces (liquisearch.com)

A document was completed, and it felt like that was it, no going home, as our contract to Queen and country was signed.

For the rest of that week, the regime continued, being run-ragged and constant lectures. There was a huge amount of gym time, swimming, and exercise, as well as marching and running everywhere. We were tested on how many sit-ups, push-ups, and squat thrusts we could do in a minute. It was carnage but we adapted to it, some taking more time than others.

Lectures continued, with learning and testing as we became prepared to go on exercise in the field. Luckily for me, as a fussy eater, there continued to be plenty of choices to refuel. Even if I had to learn to not eat too much as there was zero time to digest, whilst also having to eat faster than a pig. There was no pleasure in eating, it was a necessary function as part of our many procedures each day. The number of calories we would burn was extreme, roughly 7,000 a day so eating and keeping our energy up was essential.

In the first week of training, we witnessed constant shouting and people getting severe telling's off. We soon knew where we stood and as the boundaries and limits were pushed, some of the recruits couldn't take it and left the training within the initial week. As the second week began, I had a moment where I really considered going home. Before this, I had wavered, like I imagine every single one of the almost 60 recruits had.

The shock to the system, the complete change in everyday routines, and the beastings we were on the receiving end of from the corporals and sergeants. There was nothing enjoyable about the experience apart from the odd line of conversation with colleagues and the thought of the end goal. I missed so much about home — the simple things such as a hot bath, actually enjoying food, TV, resting, not being woken up at 5:30 am, and my family and friends.

Norman had warned me that training was brutal, but you can't imagine it until you are living it. I kept in mind that there was an end goal and wor kid got through it and was now travelling the world as a Marine. But then I faced a real test of willpower. It was Wednesday 18th February, and my beloved Newcastle United were playing Exeter in the F.A. Cup replay. Exeter's football ground was about 10 miles away from our base at Lympstone Commando.

Many of my mates were travelling down for the game and I could just imagine them in the back of a van, or on the train, having a great time with banter, beers, and the excitement of watching their home team in an important game. It was killing me to miss it, and I remember sitting on the end of my bed in the dorm, contemplating what to do. The pull of the match was like a magnetic draw that I was struggling to resist. I did resist, swallowing my frustration and repeating my future over and over in my head to try and soothe the pain of the missed game.

Instead, I listened to the match on someone's radio in the room as I ironed my clothes to precision and polished my boots to be used as a mirror, thinking life wasn't bloody fair. Not only was I missing out on one of my first loves, but if I left Lympstone, I could also get a lift home with my pals. It was a massive test for me as a young lad, who enjoyed nothing more than football, beers, banter, and being around mates. To rub salt into the wound, Exeter's ground is called St. James (just like Newcastle United's ground, St. James's Park). We got beat 4-0, two big disappointments in one night. My maturity, determination, and commitment were tested to the extreme that day.

Those early lessons of willpower and gritting my teeth through adversity, knowing that it would get better, is a mantra I've carried through my life. I've learnt a lot about mindset and it's now part of my job. When something was daunting to me, I learnt to break it down into manageable pieces and work through each step, always keeping in mind the end goal, and that things would get easier. The sense of achievement is its own euphoria and learning that at a young age, in harsh conditions, has allowed me to focus and achieve as an adult as well as hopefully help other people through my work.

I took one day at a time as a kid in the Marines, sometimes one hour at a time, never forgetting the end goal. Granted, it wasn't easy knowing that I was less than a fortnight into a 32-week training course, but I was determined to keep going.

We had been preparing for our first exercise in the field. Preparation included receiving our ration packs and organising our field equipment. The day came and we all stood in our troops. Rushing into the back of a wagon, we were driven to the local common to begin our field exercise. It consisted of teaching us how to survive outdoors, in any terrain, as a team. We didn't have tents in those days, instead we had a bivvy (bivouac) which is a waterproof sheeting that we had to erect and all huddle under for shelter with sleeping bags but no ground mat.

There was no deluxe six-man tent with a camp bed and stove in the corner to enjoy a beer by. It was pissing down with rain and freezing cold, and we had to make do with limited supplies. No fires were lit as this would be a signal to the enemy and we had to stay awake at night, on shift (sentry, as they call it), in case of attack. More likely a curious fox would be the nearest we got to an attack on the local common, but it was essential to learn the practice and regime for when we were in combat.

So, there we were in Farmer Giles's field, soaking wet, listening to a lecture on how to put a bivvy up. But the fun didn't stop there. We watched the demonstration in the daylight but had to practice at night-time in the pitch black with no streetlights, and only a tiny torch that seemed to provide as much light as a tealight candle. After setting up our shelter, the ration packs were dished out.

There was no sloping off to the local chippy during field exercise, we would be given a tightly packed box with our food supplies labelled A, B, C, and D.

A was my favourite as it included a tin of chicken curry, one of the few things I enjoyed. Breakfast would be a tin of bacon grill meat with some dried apple oats, which I couldn't eat, and a cup of coffee. Lunch would be a tin of pate with the blandest, cardboard-like biscuits you could imagine, more suitable for re-soling shoes than human consumption, alongside some dried soup. Then evening meal would be chicken curry with a bag of shitty rice. You also got some boiled sweets and bits of chocolate, that I relished and lived for. There was a tiny tin opener and condiments with the pack and a small book of matches, that never lit on the first strike due to the wind or rain, or just because they were useless.

We would be shown how to cook with a metal grid that had to be warmed through using a hexamine block, a tiny version of the firelighters you put in a BBQ. Once it eventually lit, our food would be placed in the mess tin to warm up and that was our cooking method. After cleaning all our cooking equipment, it was time to get prepared for the night, ensuring our shelter was adequate for rest and that we had recruits on sentry duty.

The training team showed us how to put cam cream on (short for camouflage cream), and had to be fully washed off the next morning, only to put it all back on once inspected. Cleaning was still as meticulous in the field as it was in the dorm, washing every single morning, using our mess tin. We had to clean ourselves in a river or use bottled water before being inspected to ensure an acceptable standard was maintained. Shaving had to be done daily, even though the sergeants had the most enormous handlebar moustaches.

I remember one time in the dorm when I was conforming to the shave rule, the lad next to me pointed out that I still had the plastic protector on the razor as I was running it over my face. I had zero hairs on my face, no bum fluff. I was so young so there was nothing for a razor to get a grip on, even without its plastic covering!

On exercise, we would get less sleep than in the dorm. When we eventually fell into a desperate slumber, we would be startled awake within a few hours with an order to get up, standing outside our bivvy, perhaps complete some press-ups or a run around the field, maybe an inspection, and then back to bed - to be woken at 5:00 am again feeling like the living dead. This torture went on for three nights until it was the end of week two, and it was back to the dorm to continue with the equally as unpleasant training. They had our lives and wanted to break us, getting rid of the weak ones.

As week three commenced, we were moved into smaller dorms; rooms of 6-8 lads. I was one of the youngest on the troop, but I was placed in a room with a lot of older men. I'm not sure if it was luck or if it was the training team's conscious decision to place me with older lads as mentors, but I will forever be grateful to those blokes. They looked out for me and helped me in so many ways, becoming life-long friends. I was a little Geordie radgie, and they kept me in line and had my back. Some of these lads were ex-police, and ex-army, all with much more life experience than me. They were a great bunch and helped keep me calm on the many bollockings I was on the receiving end of.

One of the countless times I was issued extra duties was justified. It was a time when we were all in line waiting to be inspected. The sergeant was walking up and down, inspecting every recruit. We all stood there, no doubt everyone felt the same as me, shitting themselves with the anxiety. Queued up, like lambs to the slaughter.

The sergeant came to me, and I fixed my eyes, staring ahead, feeling every muscle in my body tense. I continued to stand as tall as I could, making no movement. He leaned in assessing me, like a jeweller studying a possible precious stone, then he rammed a finger in my ear before pulling it out. The glare he gave me burnt right through me as his brow furrowed. The sergeant held up his finger and pushed it towards my eyes, a snarl on his face as he screamed,

'What the fuck is this, Stephenson, you crabby bastard?'

I could see cam cream on his finger that I hadn't cleaned properly. This resulted in extra duties for a week. I had to turn up each evening at 7:00 pm at the drill shed to do more work such as cleaning corners of the yard with a toothbrush or picking up leaves, or other degrading and demoralising tasks. The purpose was to ensure you never made that mistake again, and guess what, I've never had dirty ears again in my life. They wanted us to be blank canvases, so they could paint their own image of Marine's perfection in each of us. These brutal lessons, the oppression, and excruciating regimes, were to create flawless soldiers.

As the weeks went on, the training became more intense, physically and mentally. We continued to learn and attend lectures, finding out more about the history of the Royal Marines, map reading, survival, and weapons training. We received our SLR (self-loading rifle) as our weapon on week four and were told how to clean it, strip it down, and put it back together. At this point, we didn't fire it, but we had to know all of the many parts and it was drummed into us that our rifle was our best friend. It was not to be left anywhere. Until it was put in the armoury you didn't leave it unattended. Your weapon went everywhere with you.

Soldiering became more of a focus and the constant physical exercise continued. I can't emphasise how intense this was, it was relentless. We would be in the gym for two hours then just when we thought we might get 60 seconds respite with an unenjoyable, freezing cold shower, we would be ordered to go on a run or do 100 push-ups. It was an incessant, never-ending regime of building us up, ready for possible war.

Many were back trooped after being injured. This basically meant that if they were injured and could recuperate, they would be held back in a troop and then join the next lot of recruits at the stage they were injured.

Swimming sessions were brutal and would include swimming lengths, jumping out, putting on wet clothes, carrying bricks, treading water, and anything that sounds like hell — we were asked to do it. With progression, we all became accustomed to the routine, adapting as time went on.

Sleep was still an issue, and everyone survived on only a few hours a night, with no time to rest and relax throughout the day. It meant staying awake at opportunities where you weren't running all over the site could be problematic. This happened in lectures where sometimes the topic wasn't of great excitement, such as map reading, and we would all be fighting to not fall asleep.

Recruits are often referred to as "Nods." This is because many of us would have the body reaction of when you go to fall asleep sitting up and your head jerks in a nodding way, waking you up. After a day of getting roasted in the field with constant physical endurance on limited sleep, the lecture theatre would be full of Nods, heads bobbing up and down as all the recruits battled the desperate sleep we all craved.

Around week four, we were out on field exercise again, at a place called Woodbury Common. In a way, we knew what to expect this time, but it certainly didn't make it any easier. It was early March, and it was bloody freezing, raining and frosty, typical grim British weather. Woodbury Common was covered in prickly gorse bushes, trees, and ditches. Our tasks were to survive the outdoors, learning camouflage, map reading, inspections, and sleep deprivation.

When we returned to camp, we were allowed off camp for the first time on a Saturday afternoon. The thought of this felt like England winning the World Cup but before we could go off camp, we were inspected and, of course, we never passed the first time in case we became complacent. It meant that if we had six hours of free time that afternoon, time would begin to be shaved off and we would watch the minutes trickle away like water down the sink as we continuously failed inspection and had to start again. This could be a locker not being clean enough, anything that could make us learn more of a lesson about precision.

Another test for us recruits to see the carrot of a little bit of freedom dangled, only to be taken away. They wanted us to tell them to fuck off and say we were going home. Every single thing during every minute of every day was a test. When we eventually passed inspection, we would have to go to the guard room one at a time in our civvy clothes, ready to go out and be inspected again, having to say,

'Recruit Stephenson, permission to go ashore, sir?'

The ashore reference was from our Royal Navy connection and going ashore was used when leaving the base/ship. We would also say run ashore, which referred to going out on the drink.

After asking permission, there was a further test from the duty corporal such as having to tell him a funny joke or do a dance. If you didn't make the corporal laugh, you would be told to go to the back of the queue. Or he would tell a lad his shirt was shit and to go and change. Me being a Geordie, I was always asked to sing a song associated with Newcastle like "Fog on the Tyne" or "The Blaydon Races."

I would have to stand there, embarrassed, singing a song for his entertainment. It was degrading and another test, but if we wanted some free time then we had to do it. I would start my piece, singing the opening lines of "The Blaydon Races," feeling like a complete dickhead as I saw the shoulders of the lads in the queue moving whilst they swallowed their laughter. Then I would get a,

'Go on, you daft bastard, get on the train.'

And that was my freedom, for a few hours, at least. Freedom that tasted like the best chocolate in the world. We would get the train into Exeter, which took about 20 minutes. All of us would be dressed in shirts, ties, and polished shoes and although we looked dapper, we looked out of place in a busy town on a Saturday afternoon with most lads around us dressed in jeans and T-shirts. The other closest town was Exmouth; however, we weren't allowed to go there as many of the Marines that worked in Lympstone lived in Exmouth.

That first time "out" was a time to buy provisions and replenish our stock of items such as toiletries and pick up items we needed including knives and a decent torch. It felt strange not having to run everywhere whilst we were in Exeter, and also seeing women again, something we hadn't seen in a while but certainly hadn't stopped thinking about!

Time continued to pass, and it came to the point of us firing our rifles on week six or seven. A massive portion of us hadn't fired a gun before, unless someone had worked on a farm, or perhaps were an ex-bank robber as there were all walks of life in the recruits. I remember the kickback in my shoulder after firing the gun and everyone being in pain the next day. Lectures intensified and it was a lot to absorb, learn, and be tested on. The small advantage I had was that I had recently finished education so perhaps I was slightly more into the rhythm of learning.

The group had also spent more time together, so we had made friends, and the routine became slightly easier. In our dorm, I would perhaps polish everyone's boots as someone else ironed. We helped each other and worked together as a team. Alongside this, we were getting to know one another and finding out about each other's lives before the Marines. It was nice and helped ease thoughts of home that now and then punched me in the heart.

There were phone boxes on-site, four in total to be shared with around 500-600 people on camp. It could be two hours queuing just to speak to your mam for a few minutes, as you popped the 10-pence piece in. Conversations would be limited; I wouldn't dare tell my mam of the daily torture, and the mental and physical exhaustion. Firstly, because it was indescribable but also because I didn't want to worry her. It could be hard for us all at times, but we kept each other going with that early camaraderie.

Easter leave was coming up and I had yet to go home. There had been an option of one weekend leave previously, but given I lived so far away, it wasn't really feasible. However, we were all due our week off at Easter. Before leaving that morning, naturally, we had a beasting in the gym, running, and swimming then had to ensure our rooms and lockers were beyond perfect. The usual failing occurred until at last we were given the green light to leave for the week with the 11th-hour lesson of not forgetting the importance of being a Marine.

The train ride felt how I imagine leaving prison feels like. As we embarked, our whole being relaxed on that train, bodies melting into the carriage seat with the thought of a break from the regime. We went to the buffet cart and got some beers in, McEwan's Export. I remember giving myself a lecture to not get too many because that would make me more likely to fall asleep and perhaps miss my train stop and end up in Edinburgh. Maybe I was already growing up.

Something that I won't ever forget was the moment I knew I was home – when I saw the Tyne Bridge as our train slowed down, creeping slowly into Central Station, in Newcastle. It was like a warm hug. And when you see the bridges, you kna yer yem, (you know you're home) as we would say. My city, my Toon. I was home, for a week at least!

CHAPTER 6
IT PAYS TO BE A WINNER

Getting off the train for my first visit home since beginning Royal Marine training, I breathed in the air that felt like freedom, for a week at least. It was Friday night and after seeing my family, my priority was getting out on the drink with the lads. In particular, meeting up with my best mates Dave, John, Choc, and Baz.

There was a pub on our estate, where we would start the night, called the Seine Boat, nicknamed "The Flying Stool," so you can imagine the carry-on that happened there. For us, it was a great meeting place, and we'd have a few pints with Dave's brother, Jimmy, before heading off to Whitley Bay on the pull. Whitley Bay used to be a buzzing drinking haunt for local people and visitors to our lovely part of the world. The seaside town attracted hen and stag parties, out for a great time and great banter.

So off we headed to the coast, meeting up with more lads on the way. I thought I was God's gift, being a Royal Marine recruit, and couldn't wait to get flirting after so many weeks of not seeing and talking to women. Although I wanted to catch up with my mates, I was keen to chat up the lasses! My mates asked about the Marines which was hard to describe without it sounding like torture. I had to focus on the end goal, but I knew it was most definitely not the career for everyone.

Likewise, when I was home, Dad asked me to go to the local club, Chirton Club, with him. It was Dad's way of displaying his pride in me and showing me off to his mates, who were all asking questions, genuinely interested in the career of the young lad they had watched grow up.

The corporals had warned us not to drink excessively during our leave, with the message that on our return, we would be upping our physical and mental endurance. Of course, I was too busy having a great time with my mates to bother considering this – it was my first taste of freedom after a few months of intense training, and my extremely short hair was definitely being let down.

Being home, I adored Mam's home-cooked food that I could eat at a normal pace instead of shovelling it in faster than the speed a kettle boils. It was bliss walking around instead of moving at high speeds. Enjoying a bath, relaxing in hot water without someone screaming,

'Hurry up you fuckers!' was absolute heaven. Seeing my family and experiencing normality, it was divine.

But normality was soon over, and I knew I would be heading back to hell, my new normal. Doubt crept in; *did I really want this? Was it worth it?* I was a young lad and should be enjoying my life with an easy job, socialising with my mates, and meeting girls. All the things at home that I appreciated but took for granted, now felt like nuggets of gold that I needed to hold onto. It was another test, gifted to us by the training team like an envelope full of money covered in dog shit.

The morning of my return to Lympstone arrived and as I got to Newcastle train station, I felt the intense pull of home. My feet felt heavy, and each step towards the train was harder to take. But I was no quitter, despite feeling like it could be worse than volunteering to go back to prison. I gave my head a shake, reminded myself how far I had come already, took a deep breath, and boarded the train.

I had my Walkman and a fitness magazine for entertainment, then at every other stop, another recruit would get on. "Yorkie," who got on somewhere in Yorkshire and "Brum," at Birmingham, just like I was "George," or "Geordie," all of us nicknamed by where we were from. Seeing the lads helped ease the monumental "Sunday night feeling" and I mentally programmed myself to slip back into the regime that I knew was essential to pass to become a Royal Marine.

After the long journey, we arrived at Lympstone late at night and prepared our kit for the next morning. With each breath, I felt the sadness of being back to the harsh routines and I missed home already. But I kept reminding myself to focus on what I would get at the end, despite only being about a quarter of the way through training. Every time a thought fluttered into my brain about home, I used that mindset to remember my goal. Seeing my friends again helped, especially those I had become particularly close with; Jock, Mac, and Big Evs. They were smashing lads and it made a huge difference having them there with me, through the good and the bad.

There was another lad in our room called Carl, who always had a smile on his face and had great banter. One morning we were all startled after hearing the most horrendous noise. Hearts in our mouths, we all bolted up out of bed wondering what was going on. Looking around in the limited light, we could hear an awful squealing. It transpired that Carl, who was from a farm, had recorded pigs getting castrated and decided to play it, full volume at 5:00 am, in our room. He lay in the corner, giggling as we all almost pissed the bed whilst our pulses revved like car engines. I can still hear the hideous noise now. But it was times like that, despite the shock and horror of it, that kept us going through the gruelling training and further into our Royal Marines life.

At this stage in the training, we were still being taught how to march correctly. It was a lot more challenging than it looked. Some of the lads had the co-ordination of penguins and it could be farcical, had it not been for the fact that there was absolutely nothing funny about getting a bollocking off one of the training team.

We would change into drill uniforms, which included smarter trousers and buffed boots with shiny toecaps, for further inspections and the corporal would inspect us like a scientist inspects their research, looking us up and down, missing nothing. I would be terrified, holding my breath and not daring to move a muscle. Buttons had to be gleaming, boots had to be shiny enough for the corporal to see his face in them and if they weren't, we were punished by having to perform an embarrassing task such as running around the parade ground shouting,

'I'm a dickhead,' while holding a rifle above our heads.

Close-quarter battle in the field was also taught as our skills developed, such as speed surprise and type of action. If we failed inspections whilst in the field, there would be a consequence like our water bottle being launched as far possible by a corporal, then being ordered to crawl on our stomachs to find it through gorse bushes and ditches. The least enjoyable camping trip that you could possibly imagine.

Whilst training, if the team were not happy with the recruit's performance, or if they were feeling especially cruel, they would make us play a torturous game called "It Pays to be a Winner!" This was no game of charades or Monopoly, or a fun sport filled with laughter and slices of orange. Instead, the training team would find a hill and 60 of us had to run up and down it. On each round of running, they would reprieve five or so recruits that got back first, continuing like this until there was no one left.

It wasn't just a game of physical endurance, it was about developing mental strategy, and looking to see who was still in the game before deciding to go all out in one round or conserve energy. I'm sure the training team were laughing inside while we poor bastards almost burst our hearts running up and down a sodden hill, wishing time away as the brutal game went on for an hour or so.

Once after playing "It Pays to be a Winner!" the training team told us to pack our kit to return to camp. But instead of a van coming for us, we would be marching with our kits on our back, or "yomping," as they call it in the Marines. So, after feeling like our insides were going to drop out and our heart was surely going to explode from over an hour of running up and down a massive hill to the chants of,

'Come on you useless bastards.'

We then had to carry our back packs, weighing 70-90 lbs, for five miles. I was only 140 lbs at that time, so trudging the backpack to Lympstone when we were exhausted, sleep deprived, and hungry was the final fuck you from the training team.

These activities pushed us to the edge but none of us fell or jumped, instead we kept going, and on so many occasions we kept each other going as well. Little did I know that such physical and mental demands would be made of me in live operations in a hostile and dynamic conflict in the not-too-distant future.

Throughout these first few months of training, nothing was easy. The simplest of tasks became a process, a strict regime. Nothing was like it was at home, as the notepads we were as humans were scribbled out, erased, ripped up, and burnt. Only to be rewritten from day one, like a baby being born and learning everything about life.

As individual parts of a big machine, we all found certain things harder than others. For many, it was the physical intensity, for others it was the academic side. Some recruits found the homesickness the worse or they struggled to control their emotions — anger, fear, loneliness. People couldn't cope with the lack of sleep, the inability to eat normally, and the meticulous, obsessional cleaning of body and equipment. So many challenges.

For me, I struggled most with the admin side. Fitness was never a problem; I could be in my own world, in control, and age and energy was on my side. The admin parts of training didn't feel like this for me and were harder to manage. Things like getting my locker perfect, the ironing, the presentation – it would take me twice as long as other people. I would frequently ask the lads in my room if they thought my attempts would be enough and I was more often than not told no, it wouldn't cut it. They helped me a lot and I would make it up to them by doing something to try and assist them.

I just really struggled with some of these tasks and had such limited life experience in areas where I would have had the opportunity to learn and practice. I'd never had a job on civvy street; therefore, I never had to sort my work uniform, iron it, and get it ready. My kit was sportswear for footy and knocking about with mates on my estate.

Mam did the rest, so it was definitely my biggest challenge and something that I was always shouted at and punished for, despite my mates helping where they could.

Some of the lectures were also difficult. The Royal Marines are called the "Thinking Soldiers" and we were expected to have the brains as well as the physical presence and aptitude. At times I struggled with the academic side, but I persisted, never giving up. I would sit up all night trying to work out map reading, absorbing the information ready to put it into practice. One thing I did have in abundance was determination and a focused mindset. It helped me progress through my Marines training and throughout my career and life.

For all the ways that this early part of training felt like torture, those early formations of friendship were the fuel that kept us going. Camaraderie and banter were something we were all able to digest, unlike the food that would be splattered around the site in pools of sick! We looked out for each other, had each other's backs, and made each other laugh. This was just as important as many of the other elements of training; it's what you need whilst on tour, or in conflict. That teamwork and ability to make your troop laugh; sometimes in the darkest of times when they need it the most.

On many occasions, it's the banter that will get you through when life seems to be the harshest and most traumatic you can imagine — that camaraderie, that connection, that friendship. It will keep you going.

CHAPTER 7
MY FIRST KILL AS A MARINE

Royal Marines training progressed, and the 32 weeks in many ways felt like a lifetime of challenge but one that would hopefully lead to a great future. The regime continued, the brutality never ceasing but we grew accustomed to it. Our bodies adapted to the tiredness and aching as they grew stronger, like a puppy in its first few months of life. Our stomachs became used to eating fast, vomiting now and then as physical training snatched the satisfaction of a good meal away from us.

With all this, we were becoming the best versions of ourselves; the soldier we needed to be. Transforming into the most shaped, shiny, reliable part of a large machine.

It was around three months into training and the troop were just about marching in sync. With knowledge about our weapons and how to use them, and with developed skills in tactical training. Tactical training advancement included reading the land, thinking about movement, direction, and route. Along with camouflage, safety, strategy, and positioning with weapons. We were more competent, our skills needed to defend, fight, and survive becoming polished. Always evolving, always learning.

Inspections never wavered; at any time, we could be ordered for review. Constantly kept on our toes — we would think we were finishing after a 4:00 pm lecture, only to be ordered to do a six-mile run. Physical activity rose to a new intensity, exhausting levels, with a side order of anxiety that accompanied us continually being on alert. Our nerves were shot, and a state of adrenaline was familiar. You couldn't even scratch your ear during an activity without getting shouted at.

Once you made a mistake, you rarely made it again. It could be brutal beyond belief, but it was always for a purpose. The training team never wanted us to get too comfortable with our surroundings, instead, it was a permanent reaction to stimulation. Always alert, always ready, on repeat. As an individual, I think fear was the only thing that kept me focused at times. It made me toe the line, as someone who always struggled with concentration.

We had completed over three months of training, almost a third of the way through one of the longest military training programmes in the world. By now, the troop were more solid, those who couldn't make the grade were out. Some who were injured or were worthy of a second chance would go to Hunter Troop (back troop), allowing them another try in a few weeks.

It was announced that we would be doing gym pass out the following week. Everything was pass or fail, it was as simple as that. On the day of the test, we were marched to the gym on our well-trodden route and stood in our familiar troop in three ranks. We waited for the doors to open, used to the anxiety that we swallowed every morning with breakfast. As expected, the double doors burst open to a torrent of abuse,

'Right, you cunts, if any of you fail this, you'll be back trooped.'

With those warm words of encouragement, we all filed into the gym. Exercises began with jogging on the spot, then running around the gym and across camp before returning to the PTI's. Following the instructions for the gym test, we completed sprints, press-ups, and sit-ups, all on command. Up, down, up, down – human yoyos. It was brutal and we were all hanging out our arses, aware we were under the microscope and knowing if we were last, we would get a bollocking and face humiliation.

It went on and on, in and out of the gym, then back to climb 30-foot ropes over and over. The fourth time climbing we had to do something called a make-fast. It included wrapping our legs around the rope in a specific technique, gripping the rope, then letting go with our hands. We had to hold this position and say our name and number. This was practice for rope downs in helicopters when out in the field, in attacks and battle. After this, we were shaking like shitting dogs as we were escorted out of the gym by a PTI, clipboard in hand, who informed us we had all passed. Everyone let out held breaths and had a nano-second of relaxation.

Next was field exercise. The delights kept coming and the focus was on setting traps strategically and surviving on minimal rations by eating in nature. This wasn't skipping around a lovely meadow, leisurely snacking from an apple tree, and making daisy chains. Instead, we had a full lecture on which plants and shrubs we could eat.

As someone who didn't eat anything green, it was always going to be an issue for me. We were taught about which plants were poisonous and which were edible. All vegetation we could eat was 100% manky and I would almost say I would rather do without if it wasn't for the fact we burnt so much energy. No leaves were nice, it was just survival.

We were shown how to make traps to catch animals in the wild, likely something such as a hare or a species of bird. One of the corporals gave us a live demonstration of how to kill a chicken. In the field, we wouldn't be able to saunter off to get a burger meal from the nearest fast-food restaurant or just casually pick up an animal waiting to be eaten in the wild. We were the predator to them, the enemy, just as we would be during battle.

The corporal demonstrated the kill. Which was to break the chicken's neck and pull its head off. Everything was done so mechanically and with no emotion showed by the training team. They had to operate that way. Any sign of weakness or doubt could transfer onto us as trainees. He then showed us how to pluck and skin the chicken, cut it open and remove its insides before cooking it in boiling water. The process was rank. It was horrendous, even for someone who eats meat. We don't want to know the process before it gets on our plate. But in the middle of nowhere, where there may be a conflict, we would have to eat. We got the usual check of understanding,

'Does everyone understand how to kill and cook an animal in the field?'

'Yes, corporal,' we announced in unison.

Of course, after the demonstration, it was our turn to kill a chicken. Little did we know there were dozens of the birds running about and we were told that if we wanted to eat that evening, we had to catch ourselves a chicken. It was like the scene from *Rocky*, us rushing about trying to catch the birds. After some time, I caught one. Then I heard a bellowing from one of the corporals. I looked up and he was glaring over at a lad, shouting,

'Jones, what the fuck are you stroking it for? You're not going to shag it; you're going to eat it!'

Most of us were uncomfortable with the task. Some had worked on farms so were more accustomed to killing livestock, but most of us had never done it before. Clearly, Jones was saying his apologies to the poor bird. After laughing at Jones, I had to complete my first kill as a Marine. It was chicken broth all round and it was vile.

The whole exercise left everyone with a bad taste in their mouth but alongside the distaste of our actions, we had no herbs or spices, so the boiled chicken had little flavour. And we had nothing to wash away the feelings of the kill that gave us indigestion. I'm pleased to say I killed an animal to eat once, and I've never had to do it again.

The next morning, it was up at 5:00 am and ready for a load carry back to camp. This meant all of the webbing which included rifles, magazines containing our bullets, water bottles, and all our kit, had to be carried on our backs. Returning to camp starving and tired, everyone with one thing on their minds – Dutchy's. This was the burger stand at Lympstone Commando. They have recently retired but were part of the site for over half a century. Their burgers were like fast-food heaven, and even better, we didn't have to kill the cow for them.

Everyone was knackered, cut, bruised, and had sore feet. Nowadays there's better equipment with less discomfort but for us, we would be battered, covering our wounds and blisters in iodine, and taping our backs where we had injuries and sore muscles.

To keep us going, there was a night out in Exeter planned. We had experienced an afternoon of freedom in the town before, but now we had the incentive of an evening on the beer dangled in front of us. However, we had to get past the guard room and provide entertainment to the officers first. I was running out of Geordie songs by this time. Ant and Dec weren't a thing then, and Jimmy Nail and Robson and Jerome were nowhere to be seen in the charts, so my album of Geordie anthems had been exhausted. I had no choice but to begin on the football chants, which did the trick – providing lots of entertainment and laughs at my expense.

We headed off; me and my mates, Big Evs, Mac, and Jock. Also, a great mate Leon, who I had recently clicked with and I'm still good friends with to this day. Leon was from a similar background to me, coming from a council estate in Leicester. We all went off to paint the town red, or khaki green in our case. But on arrival, we found some of the local bars wouldn't let us in.

History and troop after troop had meant some colourful characters, deprived of women and alcohol had often caused a ruckus, upsetting the locals. Of course, there was the other side of the coin in that local bars were guaranteed to make a lot of money from thirsty Marines. Around 50 keen blokes, all wanting to consume weeks and months' worth of beer and spirits.

Some of the bouncers on the doors turned us away, tarring us with the incidents of recruits before. However, we found places to drink despite some of the local lads being hostile, thinking that we were going to try it on with the town's women, perhaps make a new girlfriend. We would strut in, as the recruits before us had, and we were competition.

Being a bunch of fit blokes, from all the beastings of personal training, perhaps we could be a bit too confident and cocky, me included at times, and this was intimidating and threatening to the town's lads. Added to this, the local women had a bit of a thing for the Marines. We were popular new faces, and we received a lot of attention. It was turf wars.

Everyone had been told under strict instructions that we were not to fight and if we did, we would be out of the Marines. So, we didn't fight, or made sure we weren't caught. A brilliant night was had by all, but everyone knew that we would have work to do on the Sunday — studying, getting our kit prepared for the next day, and so on. A never-ending list of jobs.

At this point in our training, we were getting ready for a few days of exercise — live firing of our weapons at Straight Point Ranges. We had learnt the principles of shooting and now were due to put them into practice. The Ranges were at the coast and the physical beastings didn't ease off. Whilst at the beautiful beach, the training team had us running up and down sand dunes at top speeds. Locals would be sunbathing, chilling with their loved ones and would witness us sprinting around, touching the water and back up the sand dunes as they enjoyed their ice cream or sandwiches in the stunning setting.

We travelled to Dartmoor to train for some troop and section attacks as our tactical training increased in skill. Our troop would be around 30 men and the section would consist of 10 men. Attacks were staged and we got a taste of what combat was like, using real soldiering skills. The exercises were with live rounds so it was serious and there was no room for mistakes. My attention stepped up a gear during this, knowing I had live rounds in my weapon. Real bullets were used as we could be in a real situation very soon. Doing this in week one when we were like *Dad's Army* would have been catastrophic but now we had the skills.

The training was deliberately left until we were at around the halfway point, every day a new page in a manual we were creating in our minds. Accidents do happen, even in situations such as training when a corporal is shouting commands. But the discipline we had drilled into us during the former months, the moulding of our entities, was being demonstrated and tested. No room for mistakes, I remember the adrenaline, the focus, the fear. It became part of me and part of my mind and body's function, my duty — that would eventually become almost as natural as breathing.

During this time, everyone was measured for our lovats and blues uniform which we would wear for our passing out parade. This was a milestone, and all of us felt the sense of pride that saturated the air. It symbolised how far we had come, but also gave each of us a boost and an acknowledgement that we were all important.

When we joined the Marines, in week one, we were looked at and asked general questions about our size. Then a basic uniform was flung at us as we scurried off to our dorm. Now we were being measured by tailors who had been called to the site. Measurements were taken and recorded for our own bespoke uniform. We were worthy and each of us felt a massive sense of pride that day believing that we really could make it through training to be in the world's most elite armed forces.

CHAPTER 8
THE CONSEQUENCE OF TRUTH

It was the halfway point in our Royal Marines training and as a group we had bonded in many ways. The routine had become familiar, and I knew, even as a 17-year-old, that I would never be the same person that I was when I started training. My mind had evolved in ways no formal education could have given me: my outlook, my attitude, my confidence.

Alongside this, my body had shaped into a frame of strength, stamina, and my tolerance threshold for both situations and physical endurance had risen dramatically. But we still had a long way to go, and I knew I would break and fuse back together numerous times before the end of my training.

Lectures continued on topics such as signals and map reading. NBC training commenced, which stood for nuclear biological and chemical. This was for NBC drills in case we were attacked by a threat in the field. We were given specific uniforms, including hazmat suits and masks. It was paramount we knew how to assemble and wear these safely, and we had to buddy up with another recruit ensuring full checks of one another over and over until we fine-tuned the process. Then the fun part came when we had to put our learning into real-life practice.

Everyone was marched into a concrete chamber, single file for a chemical attack. In our NBC uniform, each recruit took a space in the small chamber. A gas tablet was lit by the corporal as we remained in the room. When the space was filled with gas, everyone was ordered to take their masks off and say their name and number. The gas was barbaric, hitting our skin, noses, and throats. It soaked our eyes, making them water like a bloke who had been holding piss in all day.

Our whole bodies were stinging with the impact from the gas and there was no fresh air circulating. We all stood to attention, in increasing pain, saying our name and number waiting desperately for the order to put our masks back on. The exercise was successful, and we were freed into the fresh air. Dashing out, everyone was in agony, eyes streaming, gasping for air. We had blood red faces, and some lads were even frothing at the mouth.

The severity of activities, tasks, and assessments kept increasing. Helicopter dunker drills began, teaching us how to escape if a helicopter we were travelling in crashed or had to land in the sea. The technique entailed around 12 of us being strapped into a simulation helicopter above a swimming pool. Then we would be dropped into the water, wait until the helicopter was turned upside down, unclip our belts, and find a window to get out. As there were 12 of us and not 12 windows, we had to wait our turn before escaping with our kit.

Bearing in mind there were some big lads this wasn't as streamlined and simple as gliding effortlessly out of a window with ease — giving plenty of time before our lungs felt like they were going to shatter inside of us like a glass ornament. No, instead we had to pray no one got caught or struggled and we would have to frantically search for another exit as our pulse echoed in our ears, getting slower and slower. It was like a scene from an action film, but I survived.

Field exercise happened again, another chance to demonstrate what we had learnt in those past few weeks. The tasks were becoming increasingly hard, but we were getting stronger, more skilled, determined, and resilient. We were starting to know the training team better. Similar to school teachers (but think 20 times stricter), some were less scary and more encouraging, and everyone preferred one or two over others.

I say preferred loosely, as fear and respect were always the first emotions when you thought of the training team. They had to be role models in so many ways. But despite them still being extremely strict, as the weeks went on and we came closer to the end of the training, there were tiny glimpses of the more human side of the training team that transpired now and then. They had broken us and rebuilt us and towards the end of the training, there was more praise and encouragement.

There was something to look forward to – summer leave before our phase two training commenced. It was time for two weeks at home and we all needed it. The train ride to Newcastle was colourful, to say the least. We all got off at our various stops as the train headed further north, everyone having plenty of beers and banter on the way to their destination.

Returning home to North Shields, it was great seeing my family and mates again. The weekend was spent out on the drink and catching up with everyone. I took absolute pleasure in the home comforts and care from my mam but there was definitely a change in me when it came to keeping my room tidy and my motivation that she noticed. I was able to give her board money which was lovely for me to do.

Her son was growing up and she was proud of my progress, as was Dad. They didn't always show it with words, but I knew they were, and it was nice to go home and feel a sense of achievement, even though I knew phase two of training would be the ultimate test.

My mates saw the change in me as well, especially physically. But also, the odd words that I had begun using; some Marine terminology like "the head," which meant toilets and a pint was referred as a "a wet," due to the Marines connection with the Royal Navy. Whilst on leave, I kept training, knowing I had to keep on point for my return to camp.

The two weeks seemed to pass quicker than a game of footy and it was soon time to get the train back to Lympstone Commando. I was desperate for the training to be complete and fed up that my leave was over. Perking up slightly as the lads got on the train at their stops, we chatted about our leave and what was going to happen in phase two. We'd made it this far. The train eventually pulled up and we got the view of the bottom field on site, which was to be where we would spend most of our next phase of training. It was the obstacle course area, and this would be our almost daily workstation as we prepared for commando tests and the final tests at the end of our training.

The bottom field looked like a cruel version of the TV show, *It's A Knockout*. Filled with six-foot walls to climb, thirty-foot ropes to pull ourselves up or swing on, scramble nets, monkey bars, and high ledges. It was horrible, intense, exhausting, and never-ending.

When we thought we had completed the course there would be a simulated casualty evacuation. This involved picking up the nearest recruit, full kits on, carrying them in a fireman's lift position and running for 200 metres. It was in these instances when the corporal shouted the command where I would look around, trying to find a six-stone, five-foot lad. Realising they don't exist in the troop, I'd glance at the massive bloke next to me and think *shit, I wish I would have stood next to . . . whoever the smallest bloke was*. Usually, lads were happier than a dog with a bone to see me next to them, given I was one of the shortest!

Alongside this torture, we would visit the site's water tank. It was a 60-foot-wide tank, filled with water with a rope across. Our task was to crawl along the rope that was fixed about five metres above the water and do a regain, which involved dropping our bodies from the rope and just holding on with our arms then pulling our bodies back onto the rope, without falling in the water.

Of course, it became a pantomime as everyone fell off, full kit into the cold water, as they were screamed at. Over and over, they would go until they did it right. A reoccurring nightmare. The physical intensity was indescribable at times, and it never eased up. That heightened sense of anxiety was still with us. We could never be complacent, never weak.

We completed a lot of drill practice in the early stage of phase two, getting us ready for our passing out parade. I remember one time after regain at the water tank, we all went back to our block to shower and change for drill practice. I heard my name being shouted and this was when my world stopped momentarily as fate held the decision for my future in its hands.

The announcement said,

'Stephenson, to the troop commander's office.' It echoed down the corridor as everyone repeated it.

My mind went wild thinking *what's happened? Have I failed something?*

I was half wet and arrived at the office, where a member of the training team ordered me inside. I faced the troop sergeant who was sitting behind the desk. He was an American gunnery sergeant on secondment, a Vietnam vet who reminded me of Clint Eastwood in Heartbreak Ridge. He bellowed at me with his American accent,

'Stephenson, what the fuck have you been up to?'

His eyes fixed on mine as my heart began to race. I could feel myself getting sweaty, I knew that you absolutely never bring the Marines into disrepute.

'Nothing, sir,' I replied, my mouth dry.

'Fucking nothing?' he queried in a way that felt 100 times more terrifying than any telling-off from Dad or previous school teachers.

He pushed a letter across the desk that separated us and firmly said,

'You've been summoned to go to court. What's it about?'

I looked at the letter for a minute and swallowed what felt like a lump of concrete in my throat, before explaining that the only thing I could think of was that the letter could relate to an incident that occurred during my leave. I had been at my mate, Dave's house, and the police had arrived to arrest his older brother, Keith.

'I was in the wrong place at the wrong time, sir,' I protested, trying to stop the tremor in my voice and knowing that I could be thrown off the training for this.

My heart sank, the Marines were all I had wanted for so long, I'd worked bloody hard, and now it could be taken away from me, snatched in an instant. I froze, thinking it was game over – Stephenson lost. Then he continued, saying that as I had been summoned to court as a witness and not an alleged offender, it was different. He gave me three days of special leave to get home, get it sorted, and return to Lympstone, or there would be consequences.

I hadn't expected any of this, forgetting about the incident with Keith as soon as I'd returned from leave. I was relieved I wasn't being kicked out of the Marines, well not right now, but I was still absolutely gutted. I knew I had to go and get it sorted and in a short time frame. My head spinning like a champion skater, I went back to my room to pack.

As I was getting my belongings together, I heard another request for me to go to the office. I thought the whole thing must have been a wind-up as I headed back to the office. Halfway along the corridor, I was handed an envelope by one of the corporals and told to give it to the solicitor at court in North Tyneside.

Getting into Newcastle late that night, the next morning I went to see Dave and Keith to find out what was going on. Keith said he was being accused of assaulting a police officer. I had been there on the night and was needed in court the next day, to tell the truth. That next morning, we all went to court. I entered the witness stand, swore on the Bible, and told my account of events from that evening when I was on summer leave.

I had been heading over to Dave's so we could go to the local pub. There was a commotion outside his house, and I saw three police vans parked up. Voices were raised and around five or six police officers were running around the garden, trying to catch Keith. It was like a scene from *The Benny Hill Show*.

There was shouting, chasing, and people falling over. Finally, the police caught Keith and held him on the ground. Dave started to try and pull the police officers off his brother, as a few were holding him down. He was leaning over them, attempting to free Keith, and then more police officers started grabbing Dave.

A not-fun game of pile-on, bodies were all over and it was utter chaos. I went to try and help diffuse the situation. It was fight or flight, and my instincts were to get the police officers off Keith and Dave as it was overkill. Keith wriggled free and said he would attend the police station. It transpired they'd come to arrest him over an incident in a nightclub. However, the garden situation resulted in the police accusing him of assaulting one of them, by headbutting them. That's ultimately why I was in court and requested to attend as a witness.

The solicitor asked me under oath if Keith had headbutted the officer. I answered with an,

'Absolutely not,' and commented that their heads may have clashed but it would have been an accident given the proximity, and not intentional. The solicitor then read the document from the envelope the corporal had given me. It transpired to be a character reference from the gunnery sergeant and read,

"Recruit Stephenson is an honest and trustworthy potential Marine. He has been given special leave to represent his friend. I fully support him in this."

My shoulders lifted, and in my head I thought *fucking get in there, gunny!* He had played a blinder and it really mattered. The court was impressed but it also made me realise that the Marines must've thought a lot of me to write a character statement. It was our word against the police and Keith was found not guilty.

After court, a mate was waiting outside to take me straight to the train station as I only had nine hours to get back to Lympstone Commando. I made it, exhausted, but still buzzing from that character reference.

CHAPTER 9
"IT'S ONLY PAIN!"

After my special leave, I was straight back out in the field on reconnaissance exercises. These involved more sneaky strategies such as patrolling through the night, watching the enemy, setting-up observation posts and preparing ambushes. It was exciting stuff and felt like real soldiering. In between, we would be yomping and building up for our final tests at the end of our training.

Repeat inspections eased off and this was when the training team started to become a little more relaxed with us. Of course, we still got thrashed and beasted, but they were no longer trying to break us, now they were trying to mould us. We had proven ourselves, but we never rested on our laurels. Lectures and practice of signals, radio procedures, weaponry, first aid, battlefield care, the bottom field assault course, and regain all continued.

Speed marches would occur which included running on the flat, walking up and running down hills for up to 10 miles in full kit. Conducted in our three ranks, which would be a pain in the arse for me with my little legs. Typically, I would be next to the bloke taller than a set of ladders and have to try and keep up. We were all fine-tuning our skills, like an actor, but I imagine with much more physical pain! By now, although we were still marching everywhere we would be told to get to a certain place, from A to B, without a chaperone from the training team. Evolving to more autonomous soldiers as our skills sharpened, no longer treated like robots.

We received a welcome reward when informed that we would now be allowed to attend the pub that was on site each weekend. It was appropriately named Jollies, but we called it The Gronks Ball. "Gronks" were the local women who would frequent the pub. It was a cheap night out for locals and many of the women would get drinks from the gullible recruits hoping to get a date.

There were so many recruits going through training, all at different stages, and it meant that once allowed to The Gronks Ball, there would be a lot of men flocking around half a dozen women, like seagulls around a cafe, desperate for scraps of food or, in our case, desperate for a kiss or a future date. The women had the right idea, knowing how to play the recruits but we all had a great time with lots of banter.

Outside of the welcome social opportunity at Jollies, we had the pressure of constant testing on the bottom field. If we didn't pass this consistently in preparation for our final testing, the consequence was being back trooped, so the pressure was on. The time restrictions of the obstacles became stricter and included completing the full assault course in under five minutes, carrying your comrade for 200 metres in under 90 seconds, and regain done over the water tank the first time.

If you passed this, you would progress onto the Tarzan assault course. The name gives it away – everything in the air, ladders, ropes, bridges, all at 30 feet. It sounds great fun; however, it was anything but. Everyone quickly became aware that if we fell during Tarzan we would be out or back trooped with a broken bone at the very least, and some people had previously been seriously injured.

We started on a 30-foot tower, completing a zip wire that we called death slides in the Marines. A series of rope walks would follow, crawling up nets, and ladder walks, all at height and jumping with no safety equipment. Designed to test balance and competence at height; there was little health and safety in those days. It certainly wasn't an adventure playground.

With only a few weeks of training left we went to Poole for landing-craft training. This involved landing via a speedboat onto the beach, and Poole is the home for SBS (Special Boat Service). We jumped off and onto boats for landing and fast assaults. It was excellent, and again it felt like real soldiering at the point when we were almost at the end of our training and could soon be in real conflict.

Another phase was going to Dartmoor to learn rope climbing and abseiling. This felt like the "Gucci" Marines activities, taught by specialised mountain leaders. In addition to all the skills we learnt, as a troop we had built confidence in our abilities and each other that felt as secure as a safety harness.

A more testing exercise came next, that consisted of digging and living in a trench for a couple of days. A six-foot by two-foot wide grave dug with a shovel that proved to be as effective as a spoon where two of us had to sleep, shit, eat, and soldier from.

The days were passing quickly, and the finish line was in sight. We could visualise ourselves crossing that line and becoming Royal Marines. It was the topic of much discussion, and the camaraderie was strong. It kept us going during exercises, silently cheering each other on, the recognition of respect for each other's achievements as we passed. It was our fuel and even in our most depleted of times, we shared it with one another.

There was a task called the endurance course which we would be tested on at the end of training. This comprised of a two-mile run across rough terrain and included travelling through underground tunnels and rock pools. Our task involved ensuring everyone got through the underwater tunnel, with full kit on. Without being able to see a thing, we would have to be pushed through the tunnel by one recruit, then search in the dark water for a recruit at the other end who would pull us to safety, then repeat the process for the next lad in line.

This is probably one of the exercises that I had a natural advantage in due to only being little. The tunnels were referred to as "Smartie tubes." At the end, there was a four-mile run back to the site to finish the course.

There is a famous sign on one of the trees on the four-mile route. The sign has an illustration of a Royal Marine and the slogan "It's only pain!" It's strategically placed around 500 metres from the finish. We would see this sign and if we were on time, we would know we had made it – the final hurdle, for this part of the test at least.

On reaching camp, we'd run down to the shooting range and have to hit six out of ten targets, even if our rifle was full of mud from crawling through rivers. If six weren't hit, it was a fail. These were all practices done every other day, preparing us for the final tests that would decide whether the weeks of hell we'd endured were worth it, and whether we were indeed the best of the best.

It soon came time for our last field exercise and for us to put everything we had learnt into practice. This included section attacks, troop attacks, night raids, amphibious landings, abseiling attacks, enemy-guarded forts, prisoner taking, clearing rooms, using flares, weapons, speed marching, hostage rescuing, the lot.

We marched for miles, set up camp and the fun began. It was non-stop, full-on scenario after scenario, practicing everything that had been our lives for so long. This was real, everything we had learnt that had become second nature.

The end was approaching, and we would complete and pass four commando tests to get our coveted green beret. In between practicing for these four tests, it was drill, drill, and more fucking drill. Marching sometimes all day to get us ready for our passing out parade. It was a massive ball-ache but as our drill sergeant kept telling us, it had to be perfect because our loved ones would be there. Plus, we had to do ourselves and the Marines proud. He was right.

It was the second from last week of training, our assessment week. The first of the four tests that we needed to complete was the endurance course. I felt nervous, as if I were performing my Geordie songs on stage in front of an audience of 10,000. This was it, everything and more that we had all worked for. It was my future, my hopes and dreams, and I didn't want them to turn into a nightmare. My nerves also kicked in for my fellow recruits — I wanted them to succeed, we were already a team, and I couldn't imagine being a Royal Marine without those that had become my brothers.

I knew I had to get the endurance course right, any injuries would scupper my chances in the other three assessments. My trusty SLR rifle also had to not let me down at the end. Off we went, adrenaline pumping through us all, determination added into the mix. I remembered the techniques I had mastered as I went through the endurance course. All the mistakes I had corrected. Keeping my focus; my mindset. I made it and so did my faithful rifle. One down, three to go.

Next was a nine-mile speed march in our three ranks, carrying 20 lbs of kit and our rifle. We all looked to the left and right, giving each other an encouraging smile and,

'Let's do it,' in unison before we set off.

The view for the next nine miles was the bloke in front of me and I gave myself a pep talk to not let a gap emerge between me and the lad in front, or else it would disrupt the rhythm. I could fucking do this, I knew I could.

We set off, left-right, left-right. Marching then running, I returned to my mindset, knowing I could do it, I just had to keep up the pace for nine miles. The terrain was mostly flat but with some hills — we all kept going, working as a team. *Stay with him, stay with him,* I kept saying to myself about the lad in front. Timing was everything and relaxing my breathing wasn't easy. Then one of the corporals shouted,

'Keep it going troops, almost there.'

What felt like the weight of an elephant lifted from my chest. The corporal wasn't joking, I could see the towers of Lympstone in front of us. We needed to be under the 90-minute time limit, so had to keep going. Running as fast as we could and always keeping in rhythm, time was ticking and we were exhausted.

Then after what felt like hours and hours, we were instructed to halt. Some of the troop hit the ground, completely fatigued. We were ordered to stand to attention and have some pride in ourselves, before being told we had passed and that everyone could have a drink and relax.

After a short break, we were marched back to camp. There was a road with a bridge over that separated the countryside from the camp. In our ranks, we marched over the bridge back into the main gates of Lympstone. On our return, we were greeted by all the other recruits and Marines who gave us a round of applause. It was a magnificent moment and helped ease the pain of the nine brutal miles we had just conquered.

That evening we were all knackered but there was little time for rest as the Tarzan assault course was the next day. I didn't feel as apprehensive about this assessment. I had practiced so much and felt in control. My focus was to not fall, get injured, or get cramp. On arrival at the start of the challenge, everyone was given a little bit of rope, dipped in water which would be our handle for the death slide. I climbed the 30-foot tower and then waited for my order to whizz down the death slide, with no time to admire the view. On hitting the deck, it was straight up to take on the obstacles before the finale of climbing the 30-foot wall.

The acidic taste of pain was in my mouth and my temples were throbbing, along with my heart which was begging me to stop. But I wouldn't, I couldn't and as the cartoon slogan had told us so many times, "It's only pain!" I remember reaching the top of the wall, feeling like I might pass out, then I saw one of the corporals. He looked at me and give me a smile. *Get in there!* I thought, euphoric. I had done it, three down, one to go.

By now my state of mind was that I was so close, I could absolutely do it. Like scoring the winning penalty during the World Cup final, it wasn't going to be easy, and the last assessment was a 30-mile speed march, but I could do it. This was going to be the hardest test and we had never completed such a distance before.

The challenge was across Dartmoor in teams of five or six and we had to navigate it ourselves. As normal, it was against the clock. It was also our fourth consecutive day of assessments, and we were broken. Nine miles had left us looking and feeling like the cast of Michael Jackson's *Thriller*, and now we had more than treble that distance to contend with.

Despite our bodies being broken, our minds weren't. We had come too far to fail. It had to be mind over matter and focus and determination were something I had in abundance, even through exhaustion. I remember joking with my team that it was only 30 miles through Dartmoor, navigating ourselves with a time limit of eight hours carrying full kit and a rifle – what could go wrong.

After breakfast that morning, it was time to start. It was still dark at around 6:00 am, with shit weather, but the thought of our green beret being within reach was our sunshine. We paced ourselves, not wanting to start off too quickly, knowing we had a long way to go. Conditions weren't great and we had to be careful to avoid injury.

Checkpoints came and went. We would reassess our stock, have a drink, and go again. Everyone kept each other going, cheering one another on.

I hit my wall at around 26 or 27 miles when I thought I would collapse. The pain, the unbearable exhaustion, and the screams of every muscle in my body told me to give up. A voice in my mind was ordering me to stop. To go home. I gritted my teeth – even they were sore — and told the voice to,

'FUCK OFF!'

I kept going, as did my comrades and we could see lads in the distance who had set off before us, cheering us on. It was in sight, that finish line we had all dreamt of for 31 excruciating weeks. One of the corporals was holding a clipboard making gestures for us to hurry up as the clock hadn't stopped. We crossed the line, and the corporal was quiet for a few seconds. You could have heard the movements of a mouse in the deadly silence. Time stood still as we all felt overwhelmed by the words we were waiting to hear. Then he spoke,

'Well done lads, you are now Royal Marines.'

I let out the breath I'd been holding as my hands went up in the air. I looked at my brothers, all of us with massive smiles and watery eyes. We all shook hands and hugged one another, a shared feeling of euphoria, pride, and comradeship that I can still remember. We had done it! I had fucking done it! Ordered to line up, trying our best, our legs throbbing, we managed and stood to attention. The troop commander came along the line and gave us our green beret to try on. Pride healed every muscle in my body as we stood wearing our berets and the biggest smiles in the world. We were Royal Marines.

On return to camp, I rang my mam and told her to pack her bags to come down to Lympstone. Our troop all celebrated in Jollies. We spent the next few days preparing our kit and finalising the march for our passing out parade.

The day came, the one we had worked so bloody hard towards, and for many of us, the day we had sometimes thought would never come. Yet it arrived, and we were surrounded by our troop's family and friends. The atmosphere was filled with pride, and we were all buzzing. Mam and my sister, Julie, came down and it was lovely for my friends to meet them and for me to meet the parents and siblings I had heard so much about from my new family, 160 troop.

After the display, we marched to the drill yard where we officially received our green berets, the ultimate gift, the ultimate recognition — the recruits were now qualified Royal Marines. I went to see Leon and Evs, and asked what unit they were going to. They told me Plymouth and we grabbed each other, smiling,

'So the fuck am I! 42 Commando, here we come!'

CHAPTER 10
K-COMPANY

The time had come, it was October 1981, and I was a qualified Royal Marine. I would be going to 42 Commando at Bickleigh Barracks on the edge of Dartmoor, Plymouth. Before that, I had some leave, which I gladly embraced. It was home for a few weeks to meals cooked by Mam and nights out with the lads.

A part of me still didn't register that shit could indeed get real, and I could be on the battlefield at any time in my career. The Troubles in Northern Ireland were ongoing, and at this point the main existing conflict we could be drafted into. I was still focusing on travelling the world, seeing and experiencing new places, with the pride of achieving something that at times felt impossible.

I was a Royal Marine. I had survived one of the longest military training programmes in the world, and the buzz from that lasted throughout my leave. Family and friends were proud of me, which I soaked up gratefully. I had found my career and although it had been excruciatingly hard and I teetered on the cliff edge of failure so many times, I had bloody done it, and so had my troop. We had a rewarding career to look forward to, but first it was beers and banter with the lads at home, my original troop.

Leave was soon over, and I headed to my new unit in Plymouth by train. Achievement and excitement beamed out of me, shining brighter as the train headed further south. There was of course the anxious trepidation, given I was joining a fighting unit. Doubts had darted into my head sporadically throughout my leave and continued on the train ride to Bickleigh Barracks. *Could I handle it? Was I good enough? Would I cope?* I would soon find out.

Since I was now qualified and no longer training, I could buy a decent kit for my role in the Marines. Gone were the days of wearing the most uncomfortable of boots and poor-fitting clothes, or carrying a hessian sack with my kit in. I would have a quilt on my bed instead of a scratchy blanket that felt like iron wool against my skin. It was time to get the correct fitting, quality clothing and accessories – equivalent to a director in a smart suit, only ready for deployment instead of the office!

My new unit, 42 Commando, would mean that I would be working 9-5, Monday-Friday. Unless deployed or on exercise, technically it was like any other 9-5 day job would be regarding routines and expectations. It meant that Marines could go home if they lived locally, which I didn't and travelling home at weekends would be costly and time-consuming. I thought about it all on the train ride down to Plymouth. I was going into something that felt both familiar and unknown.

Soon I reached my destination. I had previously been given joining instructions – I would be joining K-Company. On arrival at Bickleigh Barracks, I entered the guard room, stood to attention, and said,

'Marine Stephenson, reporting for duty, corporal.'

He looked at me as if I was stupid, a roll of the eyes and a shake of the head, replying,

'First of all, you can cut that shit out. You're not at Lympstone now! Chill out, where do you want to be?'

I let my breath out and smiled.

'K-Company, corporal.'

I would need to get used to the environment at camp being less formal. I had made it, I had passed training, and proven myself. It was going to be different now. Still structured but less of an "us and them" mentality. It would take some getting used to. I was directed to my block and went on my way.

It was a Sunday evening, so there weren't many people around. Some had families in the local area, so fewer people were living there. I looked for joining instructions on the noticeboard, of which there were none. Instead, I found myself an empty bed in one of the double rooms, unpacked, and got my head down for the night, falling asleep quickly after the long journey.

The next morning I got up, put my uniform on, and went to the office. I was greeted outside by my mate, Leon Barker; I was delighted to see a familiar face. We were both called into the office, where the company sergeant major welcomed us officially to our troop.

'Welcome to K-Company, gentleman. Stephenson, you will be joining One Troop. Barker, you will be joining Two Troop. As you are aware, 42 Commando is a mountain and Arctic warfare unit and we will be deploying to Norway for training in January, after Christmas leave.'

We stood, listening intently and I could feel myself getting excited about going to Norway to train with my new unit. Then my bubble burst immediately as the sergeant major continued,

'Unfortunately, as both of you have joined the troop so late, you won't be able to go to Norway with your troop in January. Instead, you'll remain at camp until our return in March.'

And that was that. We left the office deflated, like a week-old party balloon. There was nothing we could do except mutter a disgruntled,

'For fucks sake,' as we exited.

One Troop, my troop, were waiting outside. I approached the sergeant and introduced myself to an immediate reply;

'Fucking hell, not another Geordie! Right lads, this is George, our newest sprog. I'm sure you lot will look after him.'

The lads took to me as I took to them – with ease. One of my main questions and priorities was what

Plymouth was like on a night out. I would be staying there most weekends and as an 18-year-old, I was keen to have some level of social life. They told me I wouldn't be disappointed, and they weren't wrong.

Life on the unit was much more relaxed, the levels of anxiety and exhaustion paling in comparison to training. Day-to-day life included lots of exercises, load carries, and lectures. The regime was less harsh, and we were able to show our skills and knowledge developed in training in a more relaxed, professional way without being barked at constantly. It was heaven to not have to cram food down my throat in record time or get items of kit launched across the room.

It was still regimented, it had to be. However, it was a calm, respectful environment which made for a much more enjoyable experience. The responsibility fell on us as individuals rather than being screamed at and called all the "fuckers" known to man. I may have been called a fucker on occasion, but not with the aggression we had been during training. It all made daily life great, and I was loving being part of the unit.

I attended lectures and training that the unit was completing ready for their Arctic training in Norway. As I listened and learnt, I was swallowing the frustration of knowing I wouldn't be going. The lads were buzzing, and really looking forward to it. Leon and I listened and tried to be happy for them whilst feeling slightly left out, like the last kid chosen on the school football team.

Christmas leave was fast approaching, and we were all looking forward to a break and for some of us, returning home to family and friends. Before leave began, I was called to the office. The sergeant said,

'Right, George, 29 Commando Gunners are looking for volunteers to go with them to Norway. Would you be interested?'

I wasn't sure who they were and after asking, I was informed they were an artillery unit that could sometimes be attached to the Marines for offensive fire support. They were a British Army regiment who were commando trained and we could work together if and when needed. For me, it was a no-brainer. Despite not being my unit, we could be working with them in the future. Three months on camp, or Norway with a new team — absolutely, yes, please! I left the office and Leon was outside.

'Go for it, mate,' I said with a wink, knowing he would be asked the same question.

We were going to Norway after all. A perfect early Christmas present and I started my leave with a bounce in my step. Leave came and went quickly with the usual time spent with family and friends. It was always precious time and with each visit home, I felt I was maturing.

Family and friends could see little changes in me. Likewise, all my mates were achieving new things as well; getting jobs and growing up. Our lives may have all begun going in slightly different directions but each time we met up, there were the unbreakable roots of our childhood that I knew would always keep us grounded and together.

On my return to Bickleigh Barracks in January 1982, it was time to prepare for Arctic training in Norway. Our kit was collected, and we were on our way, reporting to the docks for our journey to Trondheim, Norway. Once landed, there was a short journey on the bus to Oysand camp, which would be our base for the next few months.

On the bus ride, I was introduced to some more Marines from the other commando units who had also volunteered to join 29 Commando Gunners. There were about six of us and we also met Chris, a corporal, who would be our ski instructor.

Arriving at camp in the darkness, we decided to ditch our kit and head over to the NAAFI bar, to meet the lads who we would be training with. It wasn't the welcome we were expecting as the six of us entered the bar full of army lads and the situation could have been a re-enactment of a scene from a Western movie.

The music stopped. All pints were put down as eyes bore into the six lads hovering in the doorway of the pub. The tension could have blown the roof of the bar off, never mind the need for artillery! It felt like time stopped for a few seconds and Leon nudged me, whispering,

'Get ready, Jeff, this is gonna kick off.'

I was aware of the rivalry between the British Army and the Royal Marines but didn't think this would be an issue, given 29 Commando Gunners were attached to the

Marines. We could have stood there all night as the eyes burned into us, but we had to make a move. We were there, we were going to be working together, and we had to get on with it, simple as that. I walked to the bar, uncertain about what would happen but certain I needed a pint. Reaching the bar, a big lug of a man appeared. My heart was racing as the muscle mountain looked me up and down before barking,

'Where ye from?'

I glanced at him, heartbeat slowing slightly as I heard a familiar accent. I tried to remain cool and repeated in my head not to give him any shit. I answered,

'North Shields, just outside Newcastle. Why like?'

He nodded and replied,

'Aye, I know North Shields. I'm from Walker, just up the road from ye. Get yer beer and come and sit with me.'

And that was it, my gut stopped doing cartwheels as the blanket of acceptance covered me and, therefore, the other Marines. The music started playing again and the remainder of the night went without a hitch. We became part of the team, accepted by everyone thanks to the camp hard man who was a Geordie, thank fuck.

The next morning, we were up early, fed and watered, before grabbing some kit and skis and reporting for our first-day training. Ski Sunday it wasn't! We spent the day learning a technique called diagonal gate or stride — to ski on flat and to move uphill.

Chris, our instructor, was very experienced and a nice bloke who helped us to develop and over the next few weeks, we all became accomplished skiers. Learning was daily in order to teach us how to survive in Arctic temperatures.

Being a Geordie, I was used to the cold, but of course, this was on another level. Temperatures going as low as minus 30 degrees, meant surviving in the Arctic and freezing conditions was critical. Building shelters, for example, in such temperatures was a skill that had to be perfected. If not, it would be an uncomfortable night at best and your last night alive at worst.

Another milestone happened whilst I was training in Norway — I spent my 18th birthday in a snow hole in the middle of nowhere, freezing my tits off. Happy fucking birthday, Jeff! Norway taught me the basic Arctic survival with 29 Commando Gunners but I knew it would be harder with the Marines. However, it was a great experience, and I was grateful to get a chance to train. Even if my 18th birthday celebrations were nothing like I'd imagined a year earlier.

CHAPTER 11
THAT ISLAND OFF SCOTLAND

Norway with 29 Commando Gunners was a great opportunity, but it was nothing like my future tour experiences with the Marines. However, it was good starter practice, and I was grateful for the chance. On returning to Bickleigh Barracks, we had a couple of days back in 42, handing in our kits before it was time for Easter leave of 1982.

Leon asked me if I fancied a few nights at his home in Leicester and I thought why not. So off we went gratefully (and naively) accepting a lift from a couple of lads heading up that way. Our lift was on the back of their motorbikes and after grabbing a couple of helmets, we were ready to go.

I'm not sure how I made it the 200 miles to Leicester with my fingernails still intact, or with any of my nerves left; they'd been shot to bits during the journey. Bearing in mind what I had experienced so far in my Marines life, this was something else entirely, and an experience I have never repeated. They took no prisoners, and as we zoomed in and out of traffic at what felt faster than the speed of bullets shot from my SLR. I clung on praying we were almost there.

Eventually, we arrived at Leon's home, greeted by his hospitable mam who had lovingly prepared us a home-cooked meal. However, Leon had failed to brief his mam on my peculiar palette, and I was presented with a colourful plate of scran, served with a smile, that contained my nemesis – green stuff. Leon saw my face and not wanting to upset his mam, we tactically transferred the greens from my plate to his when she looked the other way. We got away with it, although to this day, Leon still mentions it.

With full bellies, we left for a night out in Leicester. Hitting the pubs, we had a few pints and flirted with a lass or two. Amongst the fun and games, a mate of Leon's, who was also a Marine, came over to us.

'Lads, have you seen the news?'

We both looked at him blankly, shaking our heads. He continued,

'Argentina has invaded the Falkland Islands and it looks like we may be called back to camp.'

Responding with wide eyes and,

'Fuck off, man?' I added, 'Why the fuck would they want to invade an island just off Scotland?'

I literally had no idea where the Falkland Islands were – geography wasn't my strong point, but it transpired none of us knew where the island was.

True enough, the next morning it was all over the news. I knew I had to get back to Newcastle quickly to see my family in case I was called to return to Bickleigh Barracks. Remember, in those days we didn't have the quick communication of mobile phones and email. Now if anyone is worried about someone, they can ring them. We didn't have that luxury; it was phone boxes and letters. Nor did we have the assistance of Google and online news back then. I remember being on the train, heading home, and seeing a passenger with a newspaper close by. The headline splashed across the front page:

"Argies invade British territory. Marines put on standby."

It was real. It was happening. I felt a mixture of emotions but the main one was thinking what the hell is going on. I had trained for this, we had endured the most gruelling, painfully hard training to prepare for exactly this. However, when it's real, it's another thing completely, and I stared at that newspaper headline wondering what was in store for us.

My initial concern was getting home to see my family before likely having Easter break cut short and returning to camp for deployment to the Falklands. I didn't want to call my mam; I just wanted to see her, and I knew she would be worrying about her boy.

I was 18 years old. Thinking about war frightened me, but I was also feeling anticipation and excitement. After all, it was what I'd trained for, despite not expecting to put it into practice so soon. Although I had plenty of time to think during the journey home, I still couldn't make sense of what was going to be the reality.

Arriving in Newcastle, I travelled home by taxi and was greeted by Mam on the doorstep. She gave me a long embrace. I loved my mam dearly, but we weren't the huggy type. When she grabbed me and cuddled me, like she was never going to let go, I knew something was up. She sighed and told me I had to return to Plymouth. The unit had been on the phone and the police had been around asking my whereabouts. Our unit were all over the country and world and everyone had been requested to travel back to Bickleigh Barracks, recalled for duty.

There were no trains as it was late at night, meaning I had to head back the following morning. My head was all over the place and the news coverage was focused on the invasion. Watching it, I tried to remain calm, but my insides felt like they were caught up in a hurricane. It was happening, shit, I was going to war. And I was wrong, the Falklands weren't in Scotland, they were 8,000 miles away in the South Atlantic.

The next morning, I hugged Mam goodbye. Her brows furrowed, panic etched on her face that I could do nothing about. I smiled my biggest smile and told her I would be okay; I was a Stephenson! Then I travelled back to Plymouth.

Entering Bickleigh Barracks, it was a stark contrast to the first time I arrived at 42 on that Sunday, where the place was almost empty. Instead, there was organised bustle, a hive of activity with troops getting ready for deployment. Men rushing around carrying equipment, big queues in the stores as kit was collected, lorries coming in and out of camp with supplies. Calm and controlled, but everything at pace.

I was back in my original troop, and I was put into One Section of One Troop. Our corporal in charge was a man called Kev and his two IC (second in command) was a man called Bob. The rest of my section were Jan, Gaz, Mac, Jim, Mick, and Taff. We didn't know one another just yet, but we soon would.

It was the start of April, and we had no idea when we would be heading to the Falklands. It was still sinking in for us as we got organised. There was talk going on between the nations and the UN was involved, but preparing for deployment was essential. All our kit was ready, including our Arctic kit as if we did go to war, it would be winter in the Falkland Islands and the weather was brutal.

Whilst waiting for news on the war, we spent most nights in Plymouth on the drink. After all, we never knew when it would be our last session on the beer for a long time. It was a chance to bond with my new colleagues and, of course, an opportunity to chat-up the lovely Plymouth ladies. Armed with the excellent line that I could be going to war the next day, which often worked and to be fair, was true.

It was the 8th of April 1982, the day to leave for the Falklands. Kit gathered, we marched around as K-Company, to report to the parade ground. Once we arrived, we were joined by the rest of the unit, who made up the 42 Commando. Carrying our Bergen, kit bag, and weapons, we were greeted by our commanding officer, Lieutenant Colonel Nick Vaux, accompanied by Sir Stuart Pringle, who was the commandant general of the Marines. Sir Stuart was walking with the aid of sticks, having been injured only a few months previously in Northern Ireland by an IRA bomb explosion.

Sir Stuart came to inspect us and gave a pep talk before Nick Vaux asked us to stand to attention and delivered the orders,

'42 Commando to the South Atlantic, quick march.'

And off we marched, leaving Bickleigh Barracks for the convoy of vehicles waiting to transport us to Southampton Docks where we would board our floating taxi, SS Canberra. This was a cruise ship that was being converted into a troop carrier. We nicknamed it the Great White Whale. Conversion was continuing as we embarked, with lots of modifications needed including the installation of a flight deck, adaptions to make the ship fit for purpose; fit for war.

We began boarding to the cheers, claps, and well-wishes of a huge crowd. Many family members and friends of the Marines had arrived, alongside locals wanting to show appreciation and support. I had asked my mam and family not to come down — it was a long way to travel to spend half an hour watching us, but it was nice to see people supporting us on our way.

Reaching the gangplank, it was challenging navigating the narrow entrance with all our kit. Bags were passed through first, making the process as streamlined as possible, always working together. As we boarded, cranes were lifting all of the necessary equipment for our long journey and time in the Falklands. Boarding alongside us were 40 Commando and 3 Para, plus a few other smaller units including the Royal Marines Band, who, when not playing their instruments, were medics and stretcher-bearers.

The corridors on the ship, like most cruise liners, were narrow and the layout was maze-like. Endless decks and rooms made it feel as if we were checking into a hotel on our holiday. Only we weren't on an all-inclusive to Benidorm, we were headed into the unknown, despite our extreme preparation.

Everyone congregated in a large room to be allocated our accommodation. I made my way through the maze to the cabin that would be my sleeping quarters for the next few weeks. The space was spacious and comfortable, and I would be sharing with two other lads from Signals Troop. After introducing myself, I claimed the top bunk.

Eventually, everyone was on board, and SS Canberra, our Great White Whale, set off for the 8,000-mile trip to the Falkland Islands to the tune of the Marines Band playing and the cheering, waving, and car horns of the people wishing us the best as we departed on 9th April.

It was time to get familiar with the troop carrier, our floating hotel. There was a bar on board, so naturally, we headed to explore it. The good news being it was a stylish, relaxed bar area. Rubbing our hands together we knew there would be many a great night there, until we were advised of the bad news — that we were only allocated two cans of beer a day. Only two and these weren't your big cans, they were pop-sized cans. My immediate thought was that I would need to try and source the lads that didn't drink and do some swapsies for chocolate.

Over the next few days, we settled into a routine. It included training and daily lectures on things such as patrols, attacks, and casualty care alongside lectures on the Geneva Convention and prisoner handling. Unsurprisingly, every spare hour was spent participating in extreme exercise. We would run round and round the promenade deck, often with full kit, covering many miles in our troops, day after day. Hamsters on a wheel.

Alongside this there were PT sessions, in all kinds of weather, constantly building strength and stamina. There were easily 2,000 soldiers on board, all preparing for war in the Falklands. After brutal exercise and lectures, on an evening we would go and savour our two cans of beer alongside a singsong to the entertainment provided by the Marines Band. Some nights we were allowed to go to the cinema that was on board the ship and watch a few movies, with no popcorn and hotdogs to be seen, but it was still a night out.

It was the 17th of April and SS Canberra pulled into Sierra Leone, Africa to refuel. We all gathered around the deck mesmerised by the dozens of small boats that surrounded our mammoth cruise liner. Voices shouted from all directions as the locals tried to sell us whatever was in their boat. They were basically floating shops, filled with an array of items for sale. Things you may expect such as local delicacies and handmade crafts. Then there were the more obscure items for sale, including live goats, monkeys, and even a man trying to sell his wife!

We all had a good laugh and bantered with the local salespeople, despite the language barrier, until they started trying to board the ship. As they climbed up the ladders, they had to be gently hosed to be removed from our warship. We soon finished refuelling and prepared to set off again. As we did, the governor of Siera Leone arrived with his wife and two daughters to wave us off.

The captain of SS Canberra couldn't get us away quick enough as a few suggestive gestures were aimed from the lads to the women. The captain blasted the horn as we all laughed at the childish behaviour and waved goodbye to the locals.

Back at sea, the regime of running, speed marching, heavy PT sessions, and lectures continued. I remember thinking that if nothing came of our time heading towards the Falklands, at least we would be the fittest fuckers there had ever been. Things stepped up a notch when we had to zero our weapons, getting them ready for action. Bin bags would be thrown overboard to use as targets, getting our rifles ready to shoot straight.

Then on the 20th of April, we woke up in Ascension Islands. Just past the Equator, it is a joint American Airforce and RAF base, where we had a few days to refuel. The island, mainly made up of rocks, hills, and very long roads, became the track to speed march and run on. It was boiling hot but at least it was a change of scenery.

We had some downtime on the island beaches, which were beautiful. The ocean was wonderfully warm and so clear that you could see the fish swimming alongside you. For the odd moment, it felt like paradise, the furthest away from the reality of the purpose of our journey – the horrors of war.

Soon it was time to board again and continue our journey south to the Falkland Islands. Things had stepped up a gear on the ship with the installation of GPMG (machine guns). The guns were strategically strapped around the cruise liner. We were heading towards a potential war zone and had to consider Argentinian air attacks. Then came the news that an Argentinian cruiser had been attacked, sinking with over 300 killed (The Belgrano) and one of our ships had also been targeted (HMS Sheffield) with 20 lives lost and many injured. Now there was no doubt we were going to war.

CHAPTER 12
HURRY UP AND WAIT

SS Canberra headed towards the war zone as we continued with the intensive training, preparing for what lay ahead. As our destination approached, we began unpacking and re-packing our Bergens, checking, double-checking, and triple checking. World Service news and briefings on board disseminated information, keeping us as up to date as possible. The reality of war was already with us, having heard that one of our ships was targeted and fatalities occurred. But morale was high, camaraderie kept us fuelled despite not knowing what lay ahead. Precisely what we would encounter was unknown, regardless of some of the troop's experience of previous conflicts.

I remember feeling the cool excitement in the air — anticipation alongside the adrenaline of our purpose. After a long day on board, I would relish in my rest and listen to my Walkman, with the two cassettes I had with me: one by The Human League and Meatloaf's *Bat out of Hell*, on my big 80s headphones. It offered a little normality in what felt like a surreal experience. Two pals I trained with, Lyn and Andy, managed to blag themselves a DJ slot on the ships radio station. They would take song requests, providing us all with some entertainment, although the Para's would always have to try a bit harder to get their tunes played!

As we drew closer to the Falkland Islands, briefings increased, and ammunition started to be distributed alongside our ration packs. We began packing and re-packing again, filling up our magazines with bullets. Preparing for war. Kev verbally updated everyone, advising us we were almost there. Then we received the orders for everyone to gather their kit and meet in the large hall, which was the bar area. This time it wasn't for our daily ration of two cans of beer.

I could hardly lift my Bergen; it must have weighed over 100 lbs. All of us shuffled along the corridors in silent expectation, with nods and smiles exchanged and everyone congregated in the big hall. Orders were to get ready to disembark SS Canberra, but no times were given.

Instead, we began checking each other off, applying cam cream, and waiting for further orders. Everyone tried to make themselves as comfortable as possible with our massive Bergens and holding our weapons. There were hundreds of us waiting. Time dragged, like waiting for school summer holidays when you were a kid.

I remember the sound of snoring and wondering how the hell the lads could sleep at a time like this. Then reality smacked me in the face — we were going to an inhospitable island, where the enemy was waiting to kill us — we wouldn't get anywhere semi-comfortable or safe to sleep for a very long time.

The SS Canberra had a Tannoy system that would go air-raid warning red if there was something incoming. The alert commenced as Argentinian jets headed our way. The snoozers soon woke up as eyes widened and bodies jittered. I looked around at my comrades, giving a few thumbs up and nods to my pals who I knew were thinking the same as me — how the fuck could the jets miss a massive white cruise liner sailing into the bay.

Like a natural reflex, we all put our tin hats on and prepared for an enemy attack from the jets, whilst able to do little else. Luckily, at that time, the enemy wasn't coming for us. Their targets were naval ships and although they very likely thought who the hell was going on a cruise during a conflict, the Argies couldn't have been sure that the SS Canberra was full of military personnel. The Great White Whale protected us. If the enemy had known fighting troops were on board, it could have been very different.

Kev informed us we would be moving, it was Friday 21st May and the night the operation started. We were held back in reserve whilst others made their way to shore. At first light, we received the orders to attend muster stations ready for boarding the landing crafts. K-Company was an established fighting unit with both younger and older men with a range of experience in conflict and tours. It meant that it wasn't all "sprogs" like me, thankfully.

The landing crafts were waiting — the ships that would take us to San Carlos Bay. However, transferring from a cruise ship to a fighting, landing craft was a new experience for us all. The process involved waiting to jump onto the landing deck through a narrow door. Exiting Canberra, we all made it, despite looking like tortoises with the weight and bulk of our backpacks and weapons.

The coxswain told us it was five minutes until landing. After a deep breath and swallowing what felt like a handful of sand, I looked around at my comrades, exchanging smiles and words of encouragement. This was it; the battle had begun, and we had each other's backs in whatever lay ahead. We all needed it as we entered the unknown — reassurance, support, unity.

'One minute to go,' said the coxswain, adding that he couldn't get us right to the shore, meaning we were going to get wet. Fortunately, the water was only to our knees but not an ideal way to start a war — soaking wet. It wasn't a rapid disembark, us with all of our kit, but we managed.

The Argentinians weren't expecting us on this beach and thankfully, the landing was unopposed, meaning no enemy was there. We would have been an easy target and no doubt it went through all our heads as we made our way to shore, thinking about the harrowing D-Day landings.

Orders came to find as much cover as we could, checking the area before moving around the ridge. We secured some high ground, protecting the beachhead as more of our troops and equipment landed. This would be our position for a few days, a freezing cold, wet, hole in the ground, before we were ordered to move around San Carlos Bay.

As our travels began, we came across a sheep-shearing shed. Instructed to get inside, we welcomed the relief of the warmth, the chance to make a hot drink, and attend to our drenched bodies. Many of us had soaked feet, and some lads in the troop were already struggling, the signs of possible trench foot creeping in. I removed my wet socks, squeaking against my cold skin as I pulled them off, and covered my feet in talc before encasing them in a dry pair of socks. The comfort felt like an utter luxury, all the things you take for granted that are critical out in the field.

Everything we learnt in training had a purpose. Our technique was to remove the wet socks and put them under our armpits to dry out – there were no radiators to quickly drop them over. We remained in the shed overnight, with no enemies around, and it meant some much-needed rest for us all.

The following day, we dug our trenches at a nearby ridge. This would be our defensive position against enemy attacks. Spread out in pairs, I was with Gaz, and we began digging. The ground was soft on top, with clumps of grass but became progressively harder and firmer as we dug further down. After digging about 2-3 feet deep we decided to have a break. A quick drink and a breather, the banter came straight out as we discussed how it was like digging a grave; dark humour often felt like a release.

We started digging again — stopping for long wasn't a good idea, for safety or warmth. It was winter in the Falklands and bitterly cold. Whilst digging and stopping, our sweat would begin to freeze on our faces. As we dug, enemy jets were flying overhead. We knew that they were going on bombing missions to target the ships around San Carlos Bay. However, we also knew they would return, with or without any leftover ammunition.

The troop had to get our trenches finished and position our rifles to take pot-shots at the enemy as they returned. Aware there was little chance with pot-shots against the speed of a jet, we had been taught to aim off, shooting in the path of the jet, hoping that it would travel into the bullet. It was surreal. Once the jets returned to their base and we were all okay, the digging continued until the trenches were complete.

Kev and Bob kept updating us of any news as we sat exhausted, blisters like giant marbles, covering our hands. There was little news to share, more the hurry up and wait message. Everything we had trained for over all those months and here I was, in war, digging a trench with a shovel as effective as a spoon. But the quicker we got our trench built, the quicker we could get a scrap of warmth and stay as safe as possible in our muddy ditch, getting some sleep as someone watched on sentry duty, observing for enemy attack.

The troop remained in the area for a few days before being instructed to secure one of the highest points of the island called Mount Kent, about five miles west of Port Stanley. The SAS had already been operating in the area and had numerous contacts and ambushes with the enemy. The troop gathered our kits and headed to an open space for our helicopters to land. Then the message came to stand down, we wouldn't be going to Mount Kent that night due to bad weather.

Instead, we returned to the sheep shearing shed. The place stunk. A vile, nasal cocktail of sheep shit, Marine sweat, and sodden clothes. The air was pungent but at least it was warm.

The next night, the advance was back on, and everyone boarded the troop-carrying helicopters setting off from San Carlos Bay towards Mount Kent. We left our backpacks due to weight, leaving with our fighting order – rifles, ammunition, anti-tank weapons, and two mortar bombs. Alongside my much-needed weapons, I grabbed a few dry biscuits and a packet of Nestle Rolo, not knowing when I would get some food again.

Our helicopters travelled together as a squadron. Around me, my comrades held weapons, all of us ready for battle. On landing, I remembered the heli-drills during my training and ducked down when disembarking the helicopter. If it landed on a slope, we could be decapitated.

Everyone ran for cover, spreading out, waiting, prepared for attack. We were roughly two miles away from the ridge of Mount Kent and in potential enemy territory. At this time there was a gun battle occurring and mortars coming into Mount Kent in the distance, where we were heading.

The troop began moving — alert, observing, and aware of each other's thinking, like a pack of wolves. As we walked in the damp, bitterly cold conditions, I focused on watching my step, the unforgiving terrain was another enemy and many of the lads got casualty-evacuated with twisted ankles from the boggy ground. It was pitch black, death's shadow taunting us as our heads moved in sync, side to side, looking for the enemy – an eagle searching for its prey.

Approaching the ridge, we began following the natural terrain and curve of the mountain in a traverse fashion. Flashes would illuminate the sky in the distance but were lessening, so we assumed the SAS were winning the firefight. After reaching halfway up the mountain, we saw the SAS on their descent. They had cleared the area, secured it, and advised we shouldn't have any issues.

Travelling on, we soon reached the summit and spread out along the ridge. It was very exposed, and we had no sleeping bags, no Bergens, and limited rations of food and water. Incoming mortars landed every now and then from the enemy who knew we were there.

The troop found shelter where we could. I utilised a hold under a rock — it was freezing, pissing down with rain, and I was drenched as I munched on a Rolo sweet every hour. Water bottles were soon empty. There were puddles but they were filthy, and we couldn't boil the water anywhere. Everyone drank where they could, but diarrhoea was a massive problem.

Added to this was the increasing amount of cold weather injuries inflicted on many of us. It was grim, uncomfortable, and often unbearable but we kept going – our state of mind was a weapon in itself. I tried to focus on my mindset in the most difficult of times, remembering my purpose.

After a few days, our Bergens arrived, and we were able to get our rations. These weren't the easiest to eat as many required water to make them, but we consumed the food however we could. Eventually, we left the top of Mount Kent and began our journey down, consolidated at the bottom for a few days and prepared ourselves for what lay ahead.

It's a strange phenomenon to experience and explain. We were all frightened, it's a human reaction; but that adrenalin, that resolve, made us all confident we were going to take the enemy down. Our training had changed so much about us, physically. But most of all, it had changed us mentally. It had to, we had to be killing machines and that was the reality of it.

I was only 18, perhaps the lack of experience of death in my life and lack of responsibility outside of the Marines made me less frightened. Maybe I still had that invincibility of youth. In those days, and the days that lay ahead, I lost the innocence of childhood that I still had glimmers of as an 18-year-old, even as an 18-year-old Royal Marine. Any remaining innocence froze in the bitterly cold air of the Falkland Islands as I focused on being the best man I could be, the best Royal Marine I could be.

Throughout the operations I kept thinking I didn't want to fuck up, let anyone down, let myself down. In the dark, long hours of the night, when exhaustion dominated every cell in my body, yet sleep wouldn't arrive, I would lie there thinking of home. Thinking of my loved ones, especially Mam, and knowing that being in the Falklands wasn't just about me and them. It was for all the lads around me, all the people I would meet in the future, and those I would never, ever encounter. It was for Queen and country – it was my duty.

At times, the nights dragged, and I thought the sun would never rise again as I lay awake, in the bitter cold, in the most dangerous place I had been in my 18 years. But even with the thoughts of fear, I knew I could do it. We could do it; One Section, One Troop, K-Company, our team.

We all struggled at times, but everyone helped each other in ways that could never be imagined. We were a team, a unity, and shared a bond that glued us together in our survival. We knew for certain, that what lay ahead would be the ultimate test of the strength of our survival.

CHAPTER 13
HARRIET

On the morning of June 11th, we received orders that 42 Commando were to conduct an attack on enemy-occupied Mount Harriet. I felt my chest tighten — Harriet was my mam's name, and I closed my eyes, almost trying to send her a message and hoping that Mam would be looking after me from afar as I went into battle.

The troop were a few miles away from Mount Harriet, reconnaissance and fighting patrols had already occurred to discover any enemy positions and determine safe routes. The area was filled with minefields, so it was crucial to observe the man in front as well as keep an eye out for the enemy. All of our training became apparent once more. The need for precision and teamwork, to always, always remain switched on. Perpetually reminding ourselves we could do this. We were the best of the best and had to swallow any tiny bit of doubt that we could fuck up and it could be game over.

Yomping the distance to the foot of Mount Harriet was nerve-wracking, to say the least, even before the potential battle commenced. Every step took the concentration of a tightrope walker. Brave support teams searched for land mines, creating a safe path for us.

In those days we didn't have the technology to detect the mines that we have today. It was basically a bayonet probing the area to find a safe path. The minefield was a route that the Argentinians weren't expecting us to travel, hence the decision. Instead, they assumed we would go the "safe" way and they would be waiting to ambush us — a game of cat and mouse.

Going through the minefields had obvious risks but could also, ironically, protect us. During the journey, the brutal weather sustained with freezing, soaking conditions, and challenging terrain. Sweat froze on our faces as we travelled, eyes wide, vigilant in silent solidarity.

At times managing all the factors of our environment was beyond describable but we kept going, remembering our training and the purpose of our mission. There would be the odd flare going up, the enemy searching for us as we patrolled the unexpected route. A deadly game of hide and seek as we headed towards the base of Mount Harriet.

Once we reached the holding area, we were ordered to check our kits and stand by ready for the journey up Mount Harriet. A few days before, some of the lads wrote letters for loved ones at home. They were different to the normal letters of small talk amongst the miss you messages. These were letters of the greatest love songs, words from the heart, in case they didn't make it and were killed in the conflict.

Many of the men wrote to girlfriends, fiancés, and wives. Mentioning their kids, parents, siblings — things they had to say for perhaps the last time. I didn't write a letter myself, keeping the mindset that I would be okay, I would have Mam keeping me safe from afar. For the men who did document what they needed to say, those important letters were collected and kept together to be sent, if needed.

The orders came in and were disseminated to the team by Kev. It was decided we would attack the enemy from the rear of the mountain. It would be uphill, and we were told we were likely to be heavily outnumbered. They had to be honest and prepare us, but it felt like an extra weight to carry – already a disadvantage, like a football team playing with injuries.

The odds didn't stack up but there was nothing we could do except be the strong, resilient, skilled team that we were. We were an unbreakable unit and we all silently prayed we would remain just that. As the troop were told all the disadvantages we were up against, Mam came into my mind again. I closed my eyes momentarily, *Please look after us Mam, like you always have,* I thought to myself taking a few silent seconds of reflection.

I may have been young and didn't have the responsibility of life at home with a wife and children. I hadn't the life experience and feelings of loss that many of, the mainly older lads had. In some ways I was definitely naive, in others, perhaps more blasé about it all – but I was still shitting myself and no matter how old I was or where I was in the world, my go-to comfort was always thoughts of home and Mam.

After being instructed to attack Mount Harriet from the rear, we began the journey. We knew the enemy wouldn't be expecting us to travel that route. Kit was checked again, words of encouragement shared, cam cream applied, and a quick drink of water before setting off, armed to the teeth with ammunition. I had my rifle, four magazines of rounds, a backpack full of belt links of bullets, strips of belt links across my shoulders, an anti-tank weapon which was a rocket launcher, some grenades, and flares.

I was the pack horse and then some. Kev came down the line and we had to jump up and down to make sure we didn't rattle or clunk. This was a silent attack, and any extra noise could put us at risk. I could hardly fucking move, never mind jump up and down! The call came telling us to get ready to move in one minute. We all gathered our thoughts at that minute, silent solidarity. I focused on reminding myself I could do this, we all could. I couldn't let anyone down and repeated in my head *do not bottle it, do not bottle it.*

The first part of our journey was open, and it was a clear night, making us more exposed to enemy attacks. Spreading out along the bottom of the mountain, we began our ascension in a spearhead formation. By this time the Naval Guns were battering the top of Mount Harriet. The plan as we headed up the hill, was that our navy and artillery (29, who I did my first Arctic training with alongside J-Company) would send in a barrage to get the enemy's heads down, diverting the fact we were approaching from behind and hopefully, providing us with a safer journey.

We made steady progress, waiting for the enemy. Then the artillery slowed down due to us getting closer to the Argies. It went quieter and we thought that perhaps they had done a runner. All the time the noise of my heartbeat echoed in my ears as we kept cautiously proceeding.

The enemy then set a flare off at the top of the mountain, illuminating us on our approach. Fuck, they'd seen us, and all hell broke loose. Firing commenced, the enemy pointing down at us from their trenches. An easier target as we were so much more exposed and fighting uphill. Our soldier instinct made our reactions instant, second nature for the machines we had become.

The firing continued, machine gun, rifle firing, and tracer rounds. An explosion of killing attempts. Rounds were ricocheting off rocks next to us, tracers were flying past – only visible with their colour. It was all-out war as lines and lines of rounds surrounded us. I prayed all our section were okay as my heart pounded in my chest and I swallowed fear, adrenaline making me determined and sharp.

Everyone on the ground, we aimed at the flashes flying from the enemy's rifles. Firing five or six rounds, we would hold for a second, and look around, before Kev ordered us to begin to fire manoeuvre. Move, run up the hill, firing as we travelled. Then hit the ground and fire again. All the sections took turns, supporting and protecting one another as the cascade of rounds continued to be aimed at us by the Argentinians. Knowing each other's next move, telepathic tactics of survival from the most bonded of teams.

Next, we sent some flares up, providing us with a view of where the enemy was and a target for our aim. Jan, who was blatting away on the machine gun near me shouted,

'George, pass me the ammunition in your backpack.'

'Okay, mate,' I replied as I crawled over and handed him the machine gun link, lying down as the rounds flew by.

Whilst I was in that position, with my backpack off, I decided to use my anti-tank weapon, a 66 which has a flash out of the back when used. I shouted,

'66,' warning the lads behind me to clear as they would be impacted by the flashback of the anti-tank weapon. I launched it into the enemy trench and returned to my position for fire manoeuvre up the hill. We had to keep the momentum going, keep moving, keep firing, keep protecting one another.

As we travelled, we could see the Argentinians clearer, we engaged the enemy and an intense firefight commenced. The space between us was closing in and we needed to start picking off the trenches where the enemy were, throwing hand grenades and any remaining anti-tank launchers, which were effective at trench busting. We continued to open fire as the enemy fired back, still moving towards the summit. Displays of strength, skill, and determination in our troop as we travelled towards our destination.

Eventually, we reached the top of Mount Harriet to discover bodies and kit all over the place. Smoke filled the air along with the moans and groans from the injured enemy. Looking around for movement and more attacks, searching for any enemies hiding out was paramount.

Our training had prepared us for this, but the reality is a different scenario. Many of my comrades had been in conflict in Northern Ireland and although massively different to the Falklands battle, their experience of death in war had similarities. It was new for me, for many of us, and I recall experiencing feelings of humanity at the top of Mount Harriet.

There for a purpose and part of a machine, but the human emotions were never trained out of us — they were never erased, no void left where conscience used to be. It's a battle in your own mind concerning right and wrong, good and evil, life and death. War is about defending and protecting but ultimately this often means through attack. As humans we want to protect, it's instinctive; and we did, as so many soldiers have and will continue to throughout wars. But it doesn't mean we threw our emotions away as we threw those hand grenades – we are just taught to manage them differently from civilians.

Soldiers of the enemy lay dead and dying at the top of Mount Harriet, they were humans, people, someone's father and son. I never took any comfort, elation, or glory in what I saw or did at the summit. But ultimately, they were killers and had tried to kill us all as we approached and that's what I tried to keep in my mind.

The battle wasn't over, we had to weed out the remaining enemy. This is the time that you are most vulnerable as a soldier – the last bit of the fight. It's essential to keep alert, keep looking, securing the area, clearing trenches. There was a sniper taking potshots as we covered the area. He was dealt with accordingly, then soon the enemy started to give themselves up but many still had their weapons. We were shouting,

'Levanta las manos y ríndete,' which meant put your hands up and surrender in Spanish.

Gesturing for them to get down on the ground, they were still a massive risk to us. After dropping their weapons, we gathered the prisoners so the troop could secure the area. Then the enemy began to mortar us, knowing their area had been overrun, despite being aware that their own guys were there.

The prisoners were passed to the troop ready for them at the bottom of Mount Harriet and we prepared for a counterattack as the mortar shells came in. Many of which resulted in shrapnel wounds for our men. This attack lasted around 12 hours before the order came that we would be commencing a final attack on Port Stanley, the capital, where the enemy had taken over.

A few days later the troop prepared to move to Port Stanley. After a quick drink, we gathered our kit with limited ammunition, then the message came down the line that Argentina had surrendered. We began travelling to Stanley, still on our guard, as the enemy may not have heard of the surrender.

The main officers of the enemy had surrendered to our officers, but this information may not have circulated far, meaning we were still a target. Remaining vigilant, we headed to the capital, clearing the town, ensuring the small pockets of enemy soldiers were captured.

On arrival, we began processing the prisoners with searches and I had a moment I won't forget. I still had a hand grenade attached to my kit and one of the lads noticed the pin had dropped out. Luckily, there was tape around it as an extra security precaution. It wasn't going to go off but still, it was a warning for me to stay switched on and another reminder that perhaps my mam had my back.

Processing the prisoners took hours, with everything needing to be accounted for. The Argentinians had a massive number of rations — tins and tins of corned beef. It became breakfast, dinner, and tea feeding our screaming bellies as we processed the prisoners over the following days.

The next stage of soldiers was coming in from the British Army. This was known as phase two and was planned in case anything happened to us on Mount Harriet. They were there to relieve us; the military wanted us off the island to rest after the shit we had endured.

Despite tragically losing two of our lads and 26 Marines being wounded, the battle for Mount Harriet was a textbook example of good planning - the use of deception and surprise, and the outstanding bravery and courage of the 42 Commando to overcome against all the odds. For this, the unit was awarded one DSO, one military cross, four military medals, and eight men were mentioned in dispatches. A total of 18 Argentinians were killed and over 300 were captured and taken prisoner.

For us lucky ones, we were going home, so we made our way down to the docks and onto the landing craft that had brought us into San Carlos Bay, before boarding SS Canberra. All everyone could think about was a hot shower and a warm bed. It was bliss and that first hot shower felt like the best spa experience the world could offer!

My body was sore, my mind overflowing and the realisation of just how lucky we had been out there was sinking in as I washed the battle of Mount Harriet from my skin. Of the two signals lads I had shared my cabin with on the way to the Falklands, one of them, Steve, had been severely injured. He had been saved on Mount Harriet and it was touch and go for two days.

Back on board, we had some chill time, reading the piles of letters waiting for us. I had many from my mam and friends. I read Mam's letters and couldn't help but think that she had been protecting me, all the way from North Shields.

I didn't have a girlfriend back home, but I remember as we were leaving for the Falklands, there were lots of women wanting to write to us. I recall looking through the "applicants" and, as a young lad, shallowly deciding who I fancied and wanted to write to. It was like the Premiership cards but all good fun and a kind gesture that the lasses wanted to write to us, something we were really grateful for. No doubt some of my comrades had relationships and probably marriages through these pen pals – after all, it was years before the online dating apps we have now.

Travelling to Southampton we enjoyed the relaxation and our beers. Eventually, we approached Southampton dock, where we were ordered onto the deck and a mass of small boats surrounded us, waiting to accompany us into the dock. A flotilla of hundreds and hundreds of boats sailed with us back to shore, gratitude flowing in the waves. It was a special moment and emotional for all of us, reality setting in and my heart felt bigger for our whole troop.

As we approached the dock, we were greeted by thousands of people all wanting to welcome us home and offer thanks. It was phenomenal and overwhelming but a memorable sight that gave us a boost after what we had experienced. The Falklands was a justified war – bullies taking over our territory. The public saw this and wanted to show appreciation. It was our fight to fight, and we did it.

After absorbing the gratitude, it was time to get processed. Many of us had taken "souvenirs" in the form of weapons and we had to go through what would now be a passport control system of checking bags. We called it "proffing" which meant stealing in slang. There was a wave of panic as everyone tried to dispose of their souvenirs. I had a bayonet, which I got through, but others threw their bounty in the sea. Then it was on to the coaches, to head back to Bickleigh Barracks.

During the journey, we travelled through villages where flags were on display and people boarded the bus to thank and hug us. It was incredible and everyone had a gleam in their eyes and stood a little taller. On arrival at Bickleigh Barracks, we returned all our kit. The powers that be wanted us out of the area. We were hyper and full of energy which wouldn't be appreciated in the bars of Plymouth. So, we were dispersed, and sent on extended leave.

Just my luck, there was a train strike, meaning we had to hitchhike our way home. Eventually, I made it back to North Shields. I remember arriving home in a taxi, greeted by flags billowing from the windows. I walked into the house and Mam put her hands to her mouth. She had arranged a party, but I was early. After hugs all around, and Mam holding me a little tighter than usual, my mates arrived with cases of beer, and it was a mass celebration.

I recall not long after getting home, Mam was making lunch and served up a corned beef sandwich with her usual nurturing smile. I thought she must have been winding me up, I couldn't bear to eat any more of it after living on the stuff in the Falklands. Despite always loving my mam's food, I promptly told her that I was off corned beef for the foreseeable!

In later life, especially when I became a parent myself, I've often reflected on that battle on Mount Harriet and of my mam, Harriet. How she would have felt about her son being there, knowing what was happening to a degree from the news, and no doubt her maternal instinct created all sorts of horror in her mind as she remained helpless at home. Likely thinking the worse with crippling pain that she couldn't protect her son.

A feeling I've had many times in life as a parent to my son and daughter, and no doubt will continue to feel, no matter how old they get. My mam, who didn't say much but loved us all dearly and showed it in so many ways that

I still miss to this day. The fear she must have felt, the worry.

I frequently think how it would have impacted her had I died at Mount Harriet but part of me also feels certain that Mam was protecting me there, with love that travels the longest of distance and has no geographical bounds.

CHAPTER 14
THERE FOR THE GRACE OF GOD

Following the war in the Falklands, we left Plymouth for our extended leave. Six weeks at home in North Shields, including a camping trip to the Lake District with my childhood mates. To this day, it's still one of my favourite holidays; having a laugh, drinking beers, and making memories with the lads.

The Falklands had been traumatic, and it showed in my demeanour. I had to get my head around all that had happened – process the emotions, the reality, and what could have been. As a young lad, much of this was to escape both physically and metaphorically with my mates and with alcohol used as medicine to try and forget.

Mam could see war had impacted me. Of course she could, she still knew my every reaction and personality, despite the Marines making me a precious part of their machine. One night I was struggling, and Mam came into my room. She found me crying, sweating, and shaking, as I attempted to get my head around the reality of the war I'd been part of.

It was overwhelming, haunting me at times, and in the quiet of night, it would come to me like a punch in the stomach. The rush of reality playing over and over in my mind like a horror film on repeat. The flashbacks forcing me to ruminate over the events that happened at Mount Harriet, forever etched in my memories. My body and mind reminded me of those days and processing the war took time, not just for me but for all that were there, some will still be processing it now, no doubt.

Being at home, I was grateful for the leave. However, it also meant no one was around to talk about it, no one who had been through it, who had felt what I felt, and seen what I saw. I would be having a normal conversation with my family and a memory would whoosh in, like the strongest gust of wind, targeting me, taking my breath away. Many of us would have undoubtedly experienced PTSD (Post Traumatic Stress Disorder) but of course, in the 1980s, it wasn't really a thing.

When reflecting on the battle, I knew that I could have easily been killed – one movement to the left, or one to the right and it could have been fatal. Regardless of my rollercoaster mind, I was still able to enjoy my leave, see my friends, and experience some "normality," before returning to camp.

The Marines wanted us to get back to working life and there were a lot of new faces, recent recruits who had completed their training and since joined the troop. It was the officer's job to bed the "sprogs" into the company, which meant we went back to some of the basic soldiering to help integrate the new lads. We knew from our years' planner that we wouldn't be getting deployed, so a few of us decided to find a house in Plymouth.

Myself, Leon, Trev, and Bernie rented a property in Plymouth Hoe. It became somewhere to go home each day after our shift at Bickleigh Barracks and also a party house. We would meet Fisky Pete, Karl, and the other lads who still lived on camp in town for a few pints, all good fun and hopefully we weren't too much of a nuisance as the neighbours were also participating in the party life.

We still took our jobs seriously and would run to work each morning, travelling seven miles to start our shift. The days at camp would be back to what they were before the Falklands — training, lectures, and exercises. Always keeping us on point and ready.

By now it was late 1982 and the troop were all offered some adventure training away from camp. I managed to get a place in the Lake District, perfect for being able to travel home in an hour and a half at weekends. I knew it would be a good laugh, and it was exactly that. The adventure training group were a diverse mix.

Some attended for team building from organisations, some for confidence, others were friends trying something different, and then there was me. The tasks were what you would imagine adventure training to be, including lots of water sports, raft building, camping, and climbing, with an aspect of teamwork always running through the core.

One of the tasks was to climb up Helvellyn. I remember us setting off, me carrying my own and four other people's backpacks. I arrived about an hour before everyone else and when they eventually reached the top of the mountain, I had set out a blanket and snacks for them all.

After the adventure training, it was Christmas leave, before returning in January 1983 for our annual Arctic warfare training trip to Norway. I was looking forward to the first trip with my unit. We were accommodated in lodges beside a lake and during the training we refreshed our skiing, completed basic exercises in the field, and continued to hone our skills.

One challenging task during the training was icebreaker drills. This involved cutting a square of ice from the middle of a lake. We were then faced with a ten-foot by ten-foot hole in the ice. The task was for everyone to jump into the hole and get out only using our ski poles as aids. Freezing doesn't sum it up, it was fucking torture. Luckily, I didn't have to do it for real, the practice was scarring enough. Training even included burying our shit and piss when doing our business outside. After all, anything that could give us away to the enemy was a disadvantage.

Of course, come February, it was my birthday again and another birthday in a snow hole. Welcome to being 19 years old! We did manage to have a bit of R&R in the local town, which involved too many beers and trying it on with the local lasses. It always proved quite easy for me on the flirting attempts, I hoped it was because I wasn't too ugly. But I did have to consider that the extortionate alcohol prices in Norway could have been a contributor. Even in 1983, it was around £10 a pint, so perhaps the lasses were drawn to my wallet as much as my looks and patter!

After returning to Plymouth, it was Easter leave and the usual of family, friends, flirting, and a few (too many) beers. I still didn't have a girlfriend but some of my mates did and were even looking at getting married to lovely lasses. Perhaps if I wasn't in the Marines, I may have had a relationship by this point, but I was happy to receive the odd snog and ego boost.

Alongside me doing well in my career, my childhood mates were also thriving. Dave, Baz, and John were all doing great. Many had set up their own businesses or were working for reputable companies in the area, enjoying their careers and it was great getting updates on all their achievements.

Later on, in 1983, we were deployed to Edmonton in Canada. This was to work with Canadian Special Forces, followed by a week of R&R. Another great trip, lasting around a month, allowing me to experience a different country and culture. A memorable thing about the Canadian military was the vastness of their bases. In Plymouth and other UK bases, we had the odd service such as Dutchy's, but these bases were incredible.

Similar to US bases, they were like a town. Shops, launderettes, restaurants, everything you could imagine needing and everything on a big scale. I couldn't believe the luxury and monumental size compared to our bases.

In Plymouth, we still had our rented home and on return from Canada, it was back to getting prepared for the annual Norway trip again, followed by Christmas leave in 1983. Norway was similar to previous trips, where we continued training and developing as individuals and part of a team.

This time in Norway, after celebrating my 20th birthday in yet another snow hole, we were informed we would be preparing for deployment to Northern Ireland on our return. The Troubles were still ongoing. Although the majority of severe terror attacks had happened in the 1970s, at this point, we were not aware of what the future held, and the country continued to be in a state of civil war.

We began training for Northern Ireland after a period of Easter leave, in a place called Lydd, based in Kent. It was a special unit for precise training before deployment to Northern Ireland. Here, there was a mock village where scenarios would take place and we attended lectures on explosives.

I remember all of us being in the lecture hall waiting for a session on IEDs (Improvised Explosive Devices) and a few of the chairs blew up. The team had arranged mock explosions and we were shouted at for not looking under our chairs in case of a device. We had to be vigilant, check everything at all times, starting now, as this is what we'd face in Northern Ireland.

During training, there were simulations that would involve a screen and us waiting with a rifle for "Margaret," or whoever, coming out of the launderette. We had a split second to decide if she was carrying a gun or just her laundry. Some lads would shoot, thinking she was a terrorist when she wasn't.

This was the difference with Northern Ireland – the enemy weren't soldiers, although the terrorists would have called themselves that. Instead, it was everyday people in everyday clothes, so everyone was a potential threat, a potential enemy. It was thinking about worst-case scenarios all the time – you couldn't trust anyone. Our perceptions had to alter as women and even children were a threat.

Briefings would occur on local terrorists with photos, names, and descriptions of individuals. Our job was to memorise the faces, referred to as "players." It was essential that we were aware of who they were. I took the paperwork home on leave, and it felt surreal for my mam to ask me what I was doing, perhaps thinking I was doing a crossword or reading a magazine, only to be given the reply that I was studying terrorists. These images would be embedded in our brains so that if we saw some of the players on patrol we could make it known to them that we knew who they were and would be keeping an eye on them.

On leave, I updated my parents and friends on where I would be going next. Obviously, they were concerned but I felt prepared and had experienced war before, despite the massive difference Northern Ireland would deliver. However, I still felt fear, even with the excitement of the deployment and eagerness to do my best.

The news depicted the conflict and showed the world the destruction brought on by opposing ideologies. We understood conflicts, their political and religious origins, and the way views can become something so catastrophic. We were there; the armed forces as a whole, to help. To protect, to defend.

Leave was soon over, and we returned to base to be deployed in July 1984 to the countryside of Northern Ireland. Our station was in South Armagh, referred to as "Bandit Country." Orders were to be aware of farmers as well as the local village people. Our base was an old police station in Keady, converted for our needs, to include barracks, and supplies brought in by helicopter, even though it was a working town. The town had to remain functioning, despite us being present, but we were there to do a job, to protect the innocent.

By this point, we also had new officers, sergeants, and corporals. Steve was our corporal, and he was a good lad, leading our section. Our troop was split into four groups of six people (referred to as bricks), and we all had a role on a rota basis. One group would patrol, one would be on quick reaction — ready to attend patrol where needed, another group would be on sanger duty (guarding the building including guarding towers, on the gates, watching cameras, etc.) and the final group would be resting. This routine of six-hour tasks went on around the clock. It was monotonous but essential, everything and everyone was a risk.

The sick irony of Northern Ireland was that it felt so much like home in many ways. It wasn't the other end of the world, and the English language was spoken. The everyday life that people were getting on with felt almost like North Shields or another town. We were used to wars further away, country against country, but this was different, this was a civil war on our doorstep.

We loaded our weapons and had our briefing before the first patrol went out. Everyone had to check everything around us including under cars. I remember the bizarre situation of coming out of the barracks, full combats on, weapons at hand and people just walking by going for their food shopping or on their way to work. A surreal and oppressive environment for children to be brought up around, with such fear and hate in their own country and sadly similar to many war-torn countries today.

It could have been the set of a Hollywood film, but it wasn't – it was the reality for the residents, living amongst this fear, this terrorism, and now it was our reality.

Although welcomed and appreciated by those who saw us as helping to protect, of course, we had the other side with their agenda.

Steve soon told me I would be at the front on a patrol, and I would need to chat with everyone, introducing myself throughout the town. There was a constant turnover of the military in the area, especially the army which had deployed a massive number of troops. We needed to make our presence known to the locals.

Some people were very welcoming and would chat, others were hostile and some who had an agenda were hostile to the point of attack. If we saw the players, they would naturally turn defensive and ask how we knew their names or why we had stopped them. Always presenting with an attitude, we knew their agenda but had to grit our teeth and remain assertive, professional, and calm.

Initially, we would patrol the streets for an hour and a half, then come back to base and debrief. In the sangers, we would remain vigilant of people approaching the base or for any suspicious behaviour. Much of the patrolling was in the countryside, filled with hedges which could both protect and be used for potential attack.

I remember one of the lads was victim of an unexpected attack, getting an electric shock on his balls as he straddled out onto a fence that was covered in greenery. It gave us a good laugh, to see him grab his crotch and roll around in the field. Times like that helped the whole troop's morale, not so pleasant for the lad with the burnt balls however!

One member of the section would carry an IED detector in their backpack. It would pick up the frequency of any possible device in the vicinity. The detector used to constantly go off, and we would all hit the deck and observe. However, it clearly picked up other things going on like local Mary listening to her radio, so it wasn't very reliable.

Also, within the area, there were culverts under most roads. Prime places for people to plant bombs to blow up travelling cars on the road above. On one occasion, we were on patrol and saw someone in a culvert. Making our way over to the area, we were about to open fire, but it transpired it was a glue sniffer, getting high, oblivious to the danger he had put himself in outside of the solvent abuse risk.

Another thing I recall was a lad in our troop, who was known for being a ladies' man, or a "fanny rat," as we would call him. He had managed, somehow, whilst on patrol in town, to meet a local lass and put the charm on her. The result was that every few days we would receive one of her love letters under the main doors or attached to a brick and thrown over the wall of the barracks. We took great delight in mocking the lad and informing him that a brick had arrived for his attention. I believe they carried on the relationship afterwards, so it may have been the start of the most beautiful love story. It started with a brick!

Another memory is of being on patrol when we heard gunshots. Reacting immediately, we travelled to the area and it transpired to be farmers on a duck gun-shoot.

There were no major incidents or fatalities during our deployment, but it was definitely an experience for many reasons. And ones that felt hard to process when I got home. I would observe people going about their business in my home town, like they had been in Northern Ireland but with many having ulterior, sinister motives, and I would feel suspicious. North Shields wasn't Northern Ireland, but it could have been or it could be in the future.

Returning home on a short period of leave, just like after my time in the Falklands, my mind and body showed the reactions to experiences in Northern Ireland. I was jittery and anytime I heard a door slam I would jump up, fight response kicking in. Always on alert. If a car backfired, I would dive back to the wall looking for cover. A constant state of adrenaline, eyes wide, scanning, ears pricked, predicting movements. Never discussed at the time, but now I see there were elements of PTSD manifesting in me from both conflicts I had served in.

I tried to use mindset, exercise, and the support of my comrades and family to overcome this. Ultimately, we had to get on with it. Process it ourselves, swallow it down, and "man up." But we are all human. Some of my mates noticed a difference in me and I was more aggressive when out on the drink. I never caused any major bother; it wasn't worth it for my career alone. But I was ready, a punchy little fucker if I had to be, and not very trusting of people. How could I be when I had come from a place where the killers wore jeans and jogging bottoms or a dress? Everyone was a suspect, and it took time for this thinking to ease.

It was soon time to return to Northern Ireland, after the end of my leave, and around this period the Brighton bombing happened. It was 1984 and the IRA bombed a hotel in Brighton where then Prime Minister, Margaret Thatcher, was holding a conference. Planted by one of the main players, Patrick Magee, the attempted assassination of a British government official resulted in five people being killed, including a politician.

This heightened the tension in Northern Ireland and we all had to continued being vigilant, never resting on our laurels. Our boss, Steve, asked me to take a patrol out and lead it. With me were Andy, Juan, Steve, and a few others who were great lads and I knew would have my back. It was a big deal for me, having to give orders, map read, and check the welfare of the section.

We were only to be in Northern Ireland for a few more days but on the wind down, we were most at risk. Guard can drop and the enemy knows this. We were always at our most vulnerable on those last 100 metres back to camp — we never switched off or daydreamed, not even for a second as that second could be deadly.

There were some major differences between serving in the Falklands and Northern Ireland. I was older and more mature in Northern Ireland; my skills were more defined and my knowledge more extensive. In the Falklands, there were lots of highs and lows. In Northern Ireland there was a constant heightened alert environment, every second of every day was completely unpredictable and troops only ever stayed out for short periods of time as it was mentally exhausting.

After our deployment in Northern Ireland ended, I was back on leave before Norway for Arctic warfare training again, spending my 21st birthday in a snow hole and being battered by snowballs as presents from my troop! Then on the return from Norway, it was leave for Easter, 1985 and the rest of that year included tours to Portugal and Gibraltar, both of which were enjoyable.

However, I had begun to think about my future and decided it was the right time to give my six-month notice to leave the Marines. It had been six years and I had loved my time as a Royal Marine, but I was a young lad still and wanted to try out other career options. It would also be nice to have a pint in a pub, at home in North Shields, for one of my birthdays.

I submitted my resignation with a little bit of a heavy heart but with the mindset that the world of work would offer me something else equally as rewarding. In April 1986 I was thanked for my service and left the Royal

Marines for a new life outside of the military – grateful for my time and excited for my future.

Me, Norman, and Andrew as kids

Recruit Stephenson

Lympstone Station

160 Troop Kings Squad

Royal Marine Stephenson receiving beret

Norway, 18th birthday in snow hole

Norway

Training exercise

Falklands, SS Canberra

Falklands

Falklands

Falklands

One Section, Falklands reunion

Northern Ireland

Northern Ireland

CHAPTER 15
AUF WIEDERSEHEN, PET, HEAD SOUTH

Before leaving the Marines, I had thought about working offshore on the oil rigs, and the Marines provided some courses to explore that would assist me with getting into the field. I decided I was interested in the drilling side of working on the oil rigs and although I had some transferable skills, I needed to learn the drilling technique and process. A course was sourced but funding for that year had ceased, with the hopes of the financial support commencing again in 1987.

I, therefore, returned home for a bit, with a little money in my pocket, wondering what I could do until possibly getting onto the drilling course the following year. At the time, my mate Dave, his brothers Keith and Jimmy, and another lad, Gary, were working in London on the building sites.

Dave was home one weekend and talked about London, the work, and what sounded like a cushy number. He sensed my interest and mentioned me joining them. I was very keen; a possible few months' graft with mates and digs at their house in New Cross, Lewisham. Always up for an adventure, off I went.

It was cash-in-hand building work and London felt like one massive building site at that time. Skips seemed to be a permanent feature outside of every building and there was a constant stream of work. There was a huge disparity compared to the industry in the North East, which was around shipbuilding, fishing, steelworks, and the diminishing mining industry. In London, it was a wash of money and all about erecting new buildings, refurbs, and homeowners wanting extensions. For me and the lads, it meant an abundance of work with good pay and a decent work-life balance.

A day's graft would be followed by tea out in a pub, pints for pudding, and then back to our tiny house for the five of us – the routine repeated almost daily. The house wasn't the most spacious of places, nor the most hygienic. It was a two-bedroomed property full of us pissing, shitting, and farting! But it was good times and plenty of laughs.

Additionally, for me, after a career with limited time to spend with my childhood pals, it was great working and living with the lads I had known all my life. Even the odd disagreement about who used the last of the toilet roll didn't bother me, well not for long anyway.

We met some local lads in pubs such as The Fox and The Five Bells, who became mates. They supported Millwall FC, no Toon Army fans (the nickname for our beloved Newcastle United). At the time, there were a lot of football hooligans, so we were wary of any interactions, especially about football, with competing team supporters.

However, the locals took to us, accepted us, despite our football preferences, and we all had good banter. Millwall even became our second team that we would go and watch with our new mates. Then Newcastle United would play away in London and we would see some of the lads from home – football heaven!

Work was decent and we got to know local tradesmen and businesses. After making some connections in the area, we were offered pockets of work as part of a security team at local events such as gigs. It was an easy number, and we would work the shift then have a few pints after.

I was carefree, filling my time before a hopeful career on the oil rigs, but some of the lads worked long hours and had to work in London as they couldn't get the work, or at least decent paid work, in the North East. Some of our group and other lads we met who had moved to London for work, had young families or were saving up for their first home with girlfriends and wives. They travelled to where the graft was and some of our group returned home on the weekend.

It left a few of us free at weekends to explore London. It was the mid-1980s and London was a cosmopolitan hive of diversity, with communities that were eclectic and completely new to a lad from an almost exclusively white, seemingly heterosexual, working-class community in the North East of England.

I remember one time a few of us went to the Notting Hill Carnival and it was a rainbow explosion of costumes and personalities. I watched, eyes wide — it was amazing to see different people bold in their display, and London no doubt educated me on diversity and inclusion, even back in those days.

Our happy home grew tiresome as the novelty of us all being under one small roof began to dissolve. It was cramped and, officially, all of us weren't meant to be living there. Another local lad, Mick, moved down to the area so I offered to move in with him – creating more space in the house for the rest and giving Mick a bit of company. However, he also had tiny digs, a cramped bedsit that we called the "Bat Cave."

Downstairs from the Bat Cave, lived a guy named Tony, who was in fact the person inside the famous Hofmeister Bear that advertised the Hofmeister lager in the 1980s. He was also a circus performer so would bend steel on his chest and had been a strongman, travelling the world showing off his wonderfully bizarre talents. We would watch his tricks, mouths agape, shaking our heads before a round of applause.

One time, Mick and me were getting ready and heard a commotion downstairs. There were repeated bangs and clashes and we thought someone may have been breaking into Tony's flat. Going to see what was happening, the front door of Tony's flat was locked. Figuring a burglar wouldn't have the door locked, we broke in. Tony was in the hallway having a seizure. Mick rang the ambulance as I kept Tony safe. His arms and legs must have been making the noise, lashing out all over and he could have done himself some damage, given his strength. We were there for around 45 minutes until the ambulance arrived and by this time, Tony had come around. He was disorientated and after calming down, he couldn't remember having the seizure but thanked us for helping.

A few weeks later, we had another incident in the flat, this time including the landlord who was a big lump of a man called Ali. Mick wasn't meant to have anyone else living there and each Friday, when Ali came around for the rent, I had to make myself scarce. It would be a weekly "de-Jeff" of the flat - hiding my toothbrush, work boots, and any sign of me living there – like a secret lover.

Ali must have sussed something was going on and started visiting on a Thursday, coming into the flat to have a look in each room. I would scurry around, swearing as I collected my stuff, and would take my bag of personal things to Dave and the lads' flat for the night until Ali had been and gone. It was a right rigmarole. Then one week, sneaky Ali came to the flat on a Wednesday. The doorbell rang and Mick started braying on the bathroom door, where I was leisurely having a bath after a long day at graft.

'Jeff, get the fuck out, Ali is here!' he shouted through the door.

I replied, 'Where the fuck am I meant to go?' Rolling my eyes as I jumped out of the relaxing tub and put a towel around my waist.

Mick came in and told me to go out the window onto the roof. Mouth open and shaking my head in astonishment, I gritted my teeth and followed orders, swearing under my breath, as Mick stripped off, and put a towel around his waist to pretend to Ali he had been in the bath. It was winter and I stood out on the flat roof extension of Tony's flat in my towel, nipples as hard as the bricks around me, rubbing my head as Mick made excuses about the extra toothbrush and work boots. Ali began coming every other day after that and it was the beginning of the end of my life at the Bat Cave.

During this time, I was working with another former Marine. He asked me if I fancied doing a bit of bodyguarding at night. It was a route many who left the Marines went down but I hadn't thought about it, especially being vertically challenged! After telling him I hadn't done any close protection courses, he said it didn't matter and I could still get some work. Always willing to give a new job a go, off I went to find out more.

It sounded something I could do and may enjoy, and it meant a little extra money. They started me at the bottom end of the rung, supporting shops and pubs shutting late. My role would be to accompany managers of the businesses to the nearest night safe to deposit the day's takings – sounded fine with me.

I did this for a short period of time and there were no major incidents until one night when I was accompanying an older bloke from a pub to the night safe. It was before midnight and after he gathered the takings, we began our walk to the bank. There was a group of lads waiting in the back lane and I knew they were there waiting for us – the targets with the banknotes. It was fight or flight and noticing the gang up ahead, I calmly directed the manager of the pub the other way.

We had no weapons on us, but I was aware it was likely the gang would have something — even in those days crime in London was rife, including violent crime. We turned direction and the gang began to follow us, keeping a distance but close enough for me to know that they weren't going to back off easily. I kept navigating the businessman, sneaking glances at the gang and maintaining a steady pace, shoulders back, and calm.

For around 20 minutes, they tailed us. We were in the crowded area of central London, which was a saving grace. I managed to call the security company from a phone box, advising we were in trouble, and I was told they couldn't get anyone to us for around an hour. The gang were getting closer, and we had about 45 minutes until help arrived.

By now, we were in Leicester Square, and I decided we would go into the cinema and watch a film, believing it was unlikely the gang would follow us in. We went into a screening of Top Gun – I wondered how Tom Cruise would handle this!

As we watched the film, I hoped in the meantime the gang had given up their plan to mug us. After 45 minutes, we quietly snuck out of the cinema. Scanning the area, I couldn't see the gang as we travelled back to the phone box, where the lads from the company were waiting to collect us safely. The businessman was very grateful that I kept him and his takings safe, but that was the end of close protection for me, it just wasn't worth it.

CHAPTER 16
ROUGHNECK

Not long after my Top Gun late-night date with the pub manager and a bag full of money, I called home to be informed by my mam that a letter had arrived regarding the offshore training application. I had a place on the next course, due to start in around a month. It meant auf wiedersehen to London and the lads and a temporary return to the North East before heading off to Scotland.

I left London in 1987. It had been a blast; another adventure with mates, making memories with the lads who had been my friends all my life in a new, multicultural, diverse city that had taught me loads. The banter and beer, the work and social life, the football and new friends, it had all been great craic.

But it was time to go home for a few weeks to see my family before the offshore training began in Montrose, Scotland. At this point, my eldest brother, Norman, was still in the Marines. Andrew was 18 years old and had begun an apprenticeship as a mechanical fitter, and Julie was working at Lunn Poly, a local travel agent. They were all doing well and settled, Mam and Dad had done a good job. Home for a few weeks, I was looked after by Mam and caught up with friends before the drilling course began.

The training was six weeks long and involved learning the health and safety of working on an oil rig, techniques for rigging, and all the associated processes. During this time, I stayed at a local B&B. It was a nice place, run by an older woman, with an all-you-can-eat breakfast and a home-cooked evening meal. At night times, I would have a beer or two with the lads on the course, making new friends.

Towards the end of the course, oil companies came in to meet us, searching for recruits. I was offered a job through a company called Bawden Drilling but before starting, it was essential to do a further course, offshore survival, and I completed this locally at South Shields.

After this, I joined Bawden Drilling as a roustabout on a rig called Brae-Alpha. This was the entry-level job on the drilling team, offering a hand around the rig, observing, and learning from the drilling team before joining them. The rota was 12 hours on, 12 hours off, two weeks on, and two weeks off. It was a well-paid job and meant on my return home I had two weeks to spend with family and mates and I was able to give Mam some money towards the household.

After a short period in a roustabout role, I was promoted to the drilling team as a roughneck. It was 1988 and my new job involved working on the drilling floor. One of the roughnecks was promoted to a derrickman.

He was from Chile and had found out that I had served as a Marine in the Falklands. It created instant hostility and we had a little bit of a ruckus, both with different opinions.

I remember one day, he was up on the derrick, and I was below on the rig floor, drilling. A spanner came flying down from above and just missed me. It felt like he had targeted me, but I couldn't prove it. I wasn't impressed and after another confrontation, I vowed to sort it out when we got offshore.

However, I was then promoted to a derrickman so had to work in partnership even more with the Chilean with an attitude! Obviously, I got no training from him, and he would avoid any communication with me. Instead, I was left to go up and down a huge structure, secured with rope, wondering if he had tampered with the safety harness. We never did get to sort out our differences on land as the Piper-Alpha disaster happened in the days that followed.

On the day of the disaster, we were all doing our job and one of the crane drivers came out of his machine, telling us to look over into the distance. There was a massive glow in the sea, lighting the water up for miles around. Everyone stopped work and gathered. I could feel the colour drain from my face as we all silently watched in horror as flames engulfed the area close to us, an area where we knew the Piper-Alpha rig was stationed.

Tuning into the radio channel, we heard repeated maydays and pleas for help. Panic started to show as people began to pace, asking questions, heads in hands, as our boss tried to calm the situation, claiming it would just be the flames coming from the stands on the rig (which was usual practice) and ordering us back to work. Shaking our heads, we knew something was severely wrong and refused to return to our roles, fearful for our own safety due to the rigs possibly being connected on the seabed, as well as the clear danger for our colleagues on the Piper-Alpha rig.

The emergency support began to be dispatched as we watched, helpless. Many of the lads on my rig had colleagues on other rigs, they had worked offshore for years and had moved around. Some of the lads I had trained with myself had also been stationed on Piper-Alpha. My heart was racing, I felt powerless as I absorbed the reality that it could easily have been me on that rig. Perhaps something, someone, somewhere had been protecting me again.

Survivors were brought to our rig for safety whilst emergency services dealt with the tragedy. The Piper-Alpha disaster was the biggest in oil rig history. A train of events had caused a massive explosion and it led to 165 men being killed, and a further two rescue workers dying, with many more injured. Only 61 people survived, many with life-changing injuries — both physical and mental.

It took two or three days for us to be able to leave our rig. I remember the eerie and all-consuming feeling of sadness I had flying over what was left of Piper-Alpha, a smoking shell, a graveyard. It was horrendous for all those people involved and their grieving families. The impact went far and wide – some of the lads never returned to Brae-Alpha, reflecting that it could have been them on Piper-Alpha, or that something like that could easily happen again. Families not wanting their son, husband, and dad to go back to a job which was a risk.

I returned to the rig, perhaps because I had experienced so much in the Marines, maybe my fear tolerance was lower. Perhaps my lack of responsibility at home impacted my decision or maybe I just thought my guardian angel would continue to look out for me. Whatever it was, I went back on the rigs after some leave and worked there for another year or so.

Most of the time when I was on leave, I would be cramming in football and drinking sessions with the lads. By this point, my sister, Julie and youngest brother, Andrew, were also of pub frequenting ages. We would all go out on a weekend, with our own mates and arrive back home at different times. When Norman was home, that made four of us bulldozing into Mam and Dad's house at all hours.

My poor parents, especially Mam, must have been demented with us coming in at all hours, one after the other. We would start cooking, frying pans on, toaster out, making a racket, a right mess, and probably only just evading danger on many occasions.

Mam must have gotten sick of it because she started to make us each a sandwich, plated up and covered in cling-film for us all coming in. Name tags resting lovingly on the cling-film, as we all liked different things. Our plate would be waiting for each of us at stupid-o-clock in the morning as we desperately needed the carbs to soak up all the beer. And for some reason, those sandwiches always tasted bloody amazing!

During one period of leave, I met Carol. She was a barmaid, working nights in a local pub after working a day shift at Newcastle Building Society. I noticed her straight away and felt butterflies as I approached her, pushing my shoulders back and trying to look cool. We got chatting and hit it off.

I knew she was special and asked her on a date. Luckily, the Stephenson charm worked. She was different to the women I'd met previously, in all the best ways. Carol was funny, worked hard, and her smile made my heart race. I was in my late 20s and more mature (well slightly).

It felt like the natural time for me to commit to the right lady and Carol was exactly that. We began dating and soon became an item. Falling in love was a new thing for me and my world got bigger in all the amazing ways it does when you meet someone special.

Not long after meeting Carol, I moved my job location to Morecambe Bay. It was a transfer to a gas rig as a derrickman. At the time, I had to complete a few extra courses and one of those included a five-day fire-fighting course.

Courses often felt unengaging for me, as if I was going through the motions. It was hard for me to concentrate so something had to really capture my attention and make me sit up. This course was exactly that and I was all ears from the start. It held my attention throughout, like a kid watching the latest Pixar movie. I loved it and it sparked my interest in a new career. I wanted to be a firefighter!

I looked into joining Tyne and Wear Metropolitan Fire Brigade, (now named Tyne and Wear Fire and Rescue Service), and decided to apply. I soon received a letter inviting me to start the recruitment process. At the time I was living with Carol, we were happy and enjoying life as a new couple. The fire brigade felt like the perfect opportunity to work closer to home for the first time in my adult life, after being away with my employment for 12 years.

Home was definitely now where my heart was.

CHAPTER 17
A BURNING DESIRE

When I applied to join the fire service, my older brother, Norman, also decided to apply. He was still in the Marines and submitted his notice, ready for a new career at home. On his leave, we exercised together, trying to improve our fitness and it was nice to spend time with him, working towards a shared goal. We were both already physically fit but wanted to be our very best for the fitness tests that lay ahead, as part of the recruitment assessment for Tyne and Wear Fire Brigade.

I had submitted my resignation for offshore work with the prospect of a job in my hometown for the first time in my working career. I knew getting accepted into the fire service was an intense process, but I was confident and thought if I didn't make the grade, I would simply get another job at home.

Working away had taught me so much about myself and the experiences were something that would assist me with all elements of life – things that could never be learnt from a book. For that I was grateful, and the people I met on the way had enriched my life in ways that were worth more than any wage.

However, being away from home had reached its limit and I wanted to be settled in North Shields. It was an exciting prospect for many reasons and the thought of seeing Carol, my family, and my mates more than once a fortnight brought warmth to my heart.

Celebrations such as my birthday and that of loved ones, Christmas, and other holidays that I had missed all those years — I could now look forward to at home. Even if I was on shift, I would be coming home to my own bed and most importantly, I had the love of a good woman. It was going to be something completely alien to me in many ways, but it had arrived at the right time in my life, and I was looking forward to it.

Every step of the application for joining Tyne and Wear Fire Service was processed by letters, there were no emails back then. I received my letter to commence the tests and felt a buzz, knowing this could be the start of something I really wanted.

The first assessment to pass was the aptitude test and the one that I thought I would find the most challenging out of all the assessment processes. I knew I had to make a big effort so, like a student studying for finals, I went to the library to research. The exam included questions on maths, English, and science and I wanted to do my best and after being out of education so long, the cogs of my brain needed oiling.

I was invited to Headquarters at Pilgrim Street, Newcastle, to sit the test. There were around 30 men there for the exam, there weren't any females on the frontline in those days. I was a sweaty mess as I turned the page and began the test, praying my efforts would be enough. Two weeks later, I found out — receiving the letter advising me I had passed and next up would be the physical and practical tests. I felt a glow; those hours in the library had paid off.

The subsequent set of assessments would take place at South Shields fire station and included testing to ensure you could manage heights by climbing ladders, testing motor skills and coordination through putting a pump back together, tying a basic knot and matching couplings – all whilst wearing gloves. We would also have to wear a breathing apparatus (B.A.) set. This included carrying a cylinder on our backs and a full mask on our faces. The procedure was to check we could manage breathing without panicking.

Another part of the assessment involved us going into a tunnel to ensure we could cope with a small space and weren't claustrophobic. Additionally, we all had to perform a step test with pulse recording and carry eight stone dummies to confirm we were fit enough for the demands of the role. Intense assessments but the type I thrived on, and I was wound up like a spring ready to go on the morning of the tests.

Although heavy going, I loved the assessment day, and after passing the practical and fitness requirements, the next stage was an actual interview. I had transferable skills from both the Marines and working on the rigs that I hoped would help me secure my place. It worked, I managed to pass the interview, and it meant I was within reaching distance of the finish line.

The final assessment to pass was a medical. I was fit and healthy but obviously, I didn't know what was going on inside my body so heart, hearing, sight, all of those things had to be checked before being given the green light to join the service.

Finally, after a nail-biting wait, I received the decision letter. I thought I had done okay, but you never know, and the medical could have flagged up something I was unaware of. Pacing the room, I ripped open the envelope and to my relief, I was in!

Norman had been completing assessments on a different round and had also passed. However, during both our application and assessments to join Tyne and Wear Fire Brigade, the Gulf War began. Norman was needed on standby for the Marines, postponing his joining date for his fifteen-week training course with the fire service. We would have been joining at the same time, so it was a shame for wor kid, but he did join the fire service, eventually.

My training for the fire service would begin on 7th January 1991, a month before my 26th birthday. Before starting, I visited the stores to get my kit then the course commenced in South Shields. The initial day of training soon came around. Although I had some of the first day at school nerves, I was looking forward to getting stuck into a new career that I knew I would love as well as getting to know some of the lads from the assessment more.

I arrived and went into a lecture room, saying a few, 'hellos' as I took my seat. Everyone sat waiting for the fire station officer to join us. Station Officer Ramshaw soon arrived, and I liked him immediately. He had the power of authority, border-lining put-the-fear-of-God-into-you, vibes.

Looking around I saw the faces of doom on some of the recruits. Many of the trainees had come straight from college and this was their first experience of work, and it wasn't going to be an easy ride. For me, I was used to the pressure and fear factor from those in authority – not that it made me less likely to shit myself, but I knew the craic.

So, in Ramshaw walked, looking around like a lion for its prey and he soon found it as his eyes scanned the room.

'Who the fuck cut your hair, McMillan? Your granny – did she just stick a basin on ya massive heed?' he bellowed to a lad in one of the rows who went a shade similar to fire-engine red, as we all tried to stifle giggles in case we were the next target.

The laughs continued as someone came strolling in late, newspaper tucked under his arm as if he were walking through a park to find a free bench. The bloke, Lance, had been a miner all his life and was a typical

Durham gadgie. As he casually walked in said to the whole room,

'Wey, wat time did aal yeez get here, like?'

'Who the fuck are you?' boomed Ramshaw, looking around with eyes that could spark a fire themselves at this middle-aged miner with his newspaper cosy under his arm.

'Mather, Sir,' Lance replied, looking at his boss and then his watch, maintaining a casual demeanour. 'Am on time, Sir, aren't a?'

Ramshaw looked at him with utter disgust,

'Does it look like you are fucking on time?' he asked, gesturing to the rest of us sitting in our seats, most of us covering our mouths.

'Take your fucking seat, Mather!'

Lance sauntered up to his seat and made himself comfortable, no fucks given! He was a legend by the end of the course.

The day continued and we were introduced to the course content and our instructors who were sub-officers and leading firemen at the time. The chief then came in to meet us all, but when he arrived, we all thought he was a homeless man who had sauntered in off the street.

Everyone wondered who the hell he was — this guy walking in with a uniform that looked like he had borrowed it from someone 30 years ago, who was a completely different body shape to him, and hair that looked like it had been brushed with a toffee apple. As he began talking about our future in the fire service, he sounded like he had been on the beer all night, slurring his words. I listened with raised eyebrows, pleased I wasn't in the front row as I'm sure they all got a tsunami of alcohol breath on them. It was bizarre and following his pep talk, he was off, likely bumping into the walls on his way out.

After this comedy sketch-style morning, we were given the site induction and shown where our lockers would be. Everything was at pace; it was all practice for the real job. We got straight into practical exercises and learning that first week, keeping busy, just how I liked it. Rolling the hose out, getting our uniforms on, being responsible for tasks, keeping the place clean and tidy, and learning about the future job.

Similar to the Marines, the sub-officers and leading firemen would come around and tell us the tasks hadn't been completed to a high enough standard, and that we had to do them again. It was old news to me, used to the rejection in the search for perfection, I could shrug my shoulders and get back to the task.

However, it would piss off many of the trainees — most had families to go home to and the responsibility that family involved. I would try and calm them, reiterating it was only temporary. There would be a lot of swearing as we stayed late to clean the accommodation, but the fire service wasn't trying to get rid of the weak, unlike the Marines, it was just enough to keep us on point, focused, diligent. Constant practice and perfecting the process.

As we headed towards the end of our first week of training, we became accustomed to some processes as more were introduced. Exercises included running to the swimming baths and having a session in the pool – diving for bricks, holding our breath, and such like. Procedures such as running out the hose continued daily and into the following weeks – these were the processes that could mean life or death on the job. There was no shit taken by the trainers, understandably. Anything we didn't do well enough we would have to do again and also run around the tower a few times as punishment.

By this point, Carol and I had a flat in North Shields. I would return home each night and look over my notes, telling Carol about my day. It was good to have that home environment to go back to and not be living where I was training. She was also a great help each night when I would go home with my "wet legs," (like fishing waders) which were part of my uniform and needed to be scrubbed daily. I would put them in the bath, give them a clean and wash the rest of my kit, dry, and iron it. Carol would help out and make tea before I studied. I had a great team at work, and we were a brilliant team at home, life was good.

During training, everyone was tested each Friday on what we'd learnt that week. We would all be knackered, physically and mentally, from absorbing all the information each day and studying each night. Friday morning would arrive and the whole class would be sweating like it was our wedding day, as we made our way into the classroom for the test. They weren't easy and if you failed anything, you had to do it again.

We would complete the test and it was squeaky bum time waiting to be informed if it was a pass or fail that same morning. If you didn't make the grade, you had to stay behind on Friday night and do it again. I'm not sure what would have been worse, sitting the test again or having our precious weekend hours snatched by a re-sit. Luckily, I made it through the tests so never had to surrender a Friday night although saying that, I still had to go home and sort my kit out.

Socialising continued to be a big part of my life but in a more relaxed way now I wasn't on leave from the Marines or two weeks leave from offshore, and no longer needed to cram in family, beer, and football time. I had lost the anxiety of trying to pack as much as I could into a short period of time, but it took some readjusting to chill out a little and slow down from 100 mph. I still enjoyed a few pints on a Saturday night with the lads or Carol.

My mates were starting to settle down, with their partners, wives, some having kids, but we still all made time for each other – mates for life. I hoped it was also nice for Mam and Dad to have me back home. Although Dad was still working at this point, I would pop and see my parents, often with Carol, and always be welcomed, kettle on and biscuit tin out.

In weeks two and three of training, we were introduced to more kit that were needed on the job including the fire appliances and equipment used in certain scenarios. We were taught how to climb up ladders, and lectures on the types of ladders, size, and weight.

The class was getting into a nice routine, and I remember around week four, being in the lecture room and Ramshaw coming in. He gave us all a bollocking, telling us our tests weren't as high as they had been in weeks one and two and that we were slacking. He looked at me, rolled his eyes and said,

'Stephenson, you are just fucking passing every week.'

All I could think in my head as I replied,

'Yes, sir,' was that just passing was absolute gold for me!

Another lad, Jeff Haywood, got pulled apart after getting in the 90s on the first week, then the 80s. Ramshaw blasted out to him,

'Haywood, your last score was sixty-bastard-six percent. What the fuck are you doing? Did your fatha not tell you had to try hard?'

We all turned to look at Haywood, like he was a fairground attraction, thinking *your fatha?* It turned out that young Haywood, who had just turned 18, had the fire service in his family, with his dad being quite high up.

After that, poor Haywood got the mick taken out of him at any given opportunity.

As the weeks progressed, we began to practice on the drill yard and using hydrants, learning about hydraulics, knots and lines, and pumps. Any fuck ups meant us all having to run around the tower. And there were plenty of fuck ups. I remember one time we were all sent to run around the tower five times. Swearing and moaning, off we went as a team.

There was an ex-navy lad, Roachy, who was a bit of a wide-boy or a "spiv" as we would say. We all began running around the tower and after the first time, I saw Roachy hiding behind it, out of sight of the instructors as we all circled the tower. He stood, watching us panting and sweating then joined us on the last round to look like he had run the lot. Brilliant! We were all getting on well in the squad and I had made some friends in particular Roachy, Stackas, Murph, Mick, Jeff, and Dirk.

The training continued, it was a fifteen-week course and after it finished, we would be on probation in the fire service for four years — serious business and it meant serious training. Something I was used to but perhaps had buried deep in my mind, from my Marine days. Exercise, process, strength, reaction, and attention to detail. For many it was hard. For me, I managed, but some elements were trying. I had always adopted the mindset of believing I could do it.

I still have that mindset today at almost 60 years old and as a young man, in all my careers, I wanted to do my best despite often being a joker, I knew when to be serious. I wanted to control what I could to my utmost, and I always tried to encourage and champion my peers – all one team and all needing one another, each other's fuel.

Of course, there were some knackers on the training, but they all came into their own at some point, a few by force. The fire service wanted us to succeed, it was an investment and we had taken a place on training that thousands of others had applied for. It was shaping us up, making us firefighters, helping us to protect and rescue.

The weeks continued and halfway through the training, we completed a breathing apparatus (B.A.) course at another local station. It was intense and involved practical and lecture sessions, understanding the kit, pressure systems, calculating time in smoke-filled rooms, and search patterns, to name some. Teaching was also around working in sewers and tackling ship fires.

We were tested at the end of this course, but I thoroughly enjoyed the training and it felt like things were beginning to get real. Further learning included understanding RTAs (Road Traffic Accidents, now called Road Traffic Collisions), types of extinguishers and what would be used in which scenario, breaking down doors, and first aid.

Since we were heading towards the last quarter of training, the atmosphere became more relaxed and the team were getting on well, with camaraderie in abundance. We began thinking about the passing out parade that would take place at the end of the course. It would include a parade and a big display for our family and friends, invited to celebrate with us. As the final weeks approached, we began learning about day-to-day life in a station, and what it would entail including the shift patterns.

On week 12 I was called into the office after the end of a group lecture. I was asked about Norman joining the next course and if his notice period was up in the Marines. After replying that he was, they asked if I had been stealing a copy of the weekly test sheets to give to him. Of course, I had! But I wasn't going to let them know that.

After each lecture, I had been keeping a copy of the handout and our weekly test sheets. When we would be asked to pass them to the front, I would collect them from my row and pass them down to the front of the lecture hall, minus one, snaffling a copy to give to wor kid. They had eventually clicked on that one was missing but, of course, couldn't prove it. Keeping a straight face and maintaining eye contact, I denied the theft. They tried to get the truth out of me in a banter-filled way, but I kept on denying it, shaking my head, before being told to fuck off out of the office. After that, they began giving me an extra handout at the end of each lecture with a,

'There's one for your kid.'

They must have appreciated my teamwork ethic.

During our passing out parade, we would complete a drill, a presentation and receive our certification. There were several awards given out – top arse-licker and all that. One award was the silver axe award and my mate, Stackas, was given this. However, he broke his ankle playing football so was in crutches at the passing out parade and couldn't participate in the drills.

Carol and my mam came to watch my passing out and then we all went on the drink. It was a real buzz for me and symbolised the start of a new career that I was eager to begin, even more so after the training. We had registered our preferences of stations, so I chose the ones nearest to home: Tynemouth, Whitley Bay, and Wallsend. I was given Pilgrim Street, Newcastle City Centre. I remember thinking *bloody hell, how did that happen?* But it transpired to be the best thing ever.

CHAPTER 18
DELTA GREEN

I was beginning my first job with Tyne and Wear Fire Service at Delta (Pilgrim Street, Newcastle), one of the busiest stations in the area. I would be on Green watch and my start date was a week away. Before starting, I visited the station and introduced myself.

Meeting the boss, or gaffer as we referred to him, Alan, along with Brendan and Ian, the two sub-officers, and the two leading firefighters, Sandy and Kenny. The crew, who were a great bunch, were made up of Paul, Ray, Jeff, Charlie, Peter, Larry, Stevie, and Niall. We also had Rab on the team, who took over from Brendan at a later date.

I was shown around, taken to where my locker would be and generally welcomed to the station, making me immediately feel part of the team. The station I was joining was in the very centre of Newcastle, amongst office buildings, restaurants, bars, and shops. Within the station, there were two fire engines: a category one (Delta One), a category two (Delta Two), as well as an emergency tender (Delta Four).

185

Our watch was large so there would be around 13-14 of us with an extra leave group of 3-4 out at any one time. The shift pattern was two-day shifts, two-night shifts, followed by four days off – a rota with four different shifts and watches.

My first day soon arrived and off I went as a "proby." Alan came for a chat and told me he was there if I needed him, but he would let me get on with it — just what I liked. My shift started at 9:00 am, I met all the lads and was told as a proby that I would be assigned the category one vehicle with the crew.

Category one would be used for a main job and would attend to jobs such as house fires and car crashes (with category two likely attending also). Category two was used for smaller jobs such as bin fires and small car accidents. The emergency tender would be for more severe, or larger jobs — critical situations as it holds the cutting equipment and associated machines. Category three vehicles had a turntable ladder, but we didn't have one of those at Pilgrim Street.

As a new member of the watch, I was to sit in the middle, of the back of the vehicle, in between two breathing apparatus wearers but would not yet be allowed to enter a burning building until completing my induction. I was informed the jobs would come in, or as it was referred to, "the bells going down." Jobs would come through a printer and someone, usually the proby, would be responsible for taking it from the printer as the crew got ready to mobilise. The job would state persons reported if people were involved.

Not long into my shift, the first job came in, category one – full emergency at the airport, an aircraft had lost power in one engine. Off we went in Delta One, all kit on. I was sitting in the middle of two experienced firefighters, adrenaline rushing through my body as the lads on either side of me sat calmly. I asked if they had received many of these calls before and they replied that it happened all the time.

Rubbing my hands together, I was buzzing with the anticipation of helping the lads with the job and then about five minutes before we reached Newcastle Airport, it came over the radio to stand down, the plane had landed safely. Relieved no one was injured but feeling my own fire had been extinguished, I looked at my colleagues who said it was a common occurrence and precautionary in case there was a problem with the plane on landing.

That afternoon, there was another job for Delta One and Delta Two at a local metro station where a man was stuck under the train. We arrived at Benton Metro Station with our first aid packs and cutting equipment. Switching off all the electricity and evacuating the station of people, we began to investigate. It was a fatality — an old man who had either fallen or jumped onto the track and had been hit by an oncoming train.

I remember my sub-officer, Ian, asking me to pick up the deceased man's false teeth and bag them before helping the team wash away the blood. I did so, having a quiet moment as I collected the poor man's teeth and reflected that you never know someone's story. That was day one, not the most pleasant but the reality of what the fire service and many other emergency services deal with daily, and definitely an indication of things to come in my career with Tyne and Wear Fire Brigade.

I went home and talked to Carol about my day, as I did numerous times over the years, her often being my support. She would listen with intent, consideration, and compassion, helping me process events of the day. Even as I got used to the occupation and all the jobs, many of which were horrendous and will never leave me, I could process them, but I never became desensitized.

I frequently thought about the suffering and the people left behind after a fatality. Jobs stayed with you, and I often used my journey home, driving in silence, to process. You have to care in that role, like in numerous other professions. If you don't, it's not the job for you. A good firefighter isn't in it for the money, they want to help and make a difference, and they do in so many ways.

I began the night shift of my first shift pattern, starting at 6:00 pm. After parading, we would be informed of which appliance we would be on. For me, it was on Delta Two. Each shift, we had to check our kit and the machines, and then some lads could go into the gym. Jobs such as fire safety checks on nearby pubs, responding to any jobs coming in, and other checks would be part of our shift routine. Night-time brought incidents such as house fires and road traffic accidents (RTAs), especially involving drunk drivers.

The first job that came in that night was an RTA in the city centre, on the Central Motorway. The printout indicated that there had been a head-on collision. Off we went as a watch and quickly arrived at the scene of the crash, where two cars had collided. One car wasn't too severely damaged, the other didn't come off as lightly and had been crushed in parts. Our role was to cut the driver out of the smashed-up vehicle.

As a new member of the watch, I wasn't ready to assist with the cutting. Instead, my job was to support from inside the vehicle, with focus on the injured driver. I squeezed inside the car and casualty-handled the driver by opening his airways and keeping his head straight behind him. Checking for major injuries, he had significant wounds from the car crushing into his body.

The team went to work, removing parts of the damaged vehicle methodically, in order to safely free the driver as quickly as possible with minimal disruption. The spreaders and cutters were used to get the door off, remove the glass, and get to the injured driver in order to free him.

As I sat with the driver, I realised at that moment that I had joined an exceptional team. The gaffer didn't have to say much, the team just got on with what they needed to do, safely and promptly, in sync with one another —

all working towards the same goal. I kept focused on keeping the man's airways open and explaining what was happening, my voice steady, trying to keep him calm and reassuring him. I didn't feel panic, just a real determination to get the end result all my team desired.

Within around 20 minutes, the car was stripped, and we could move the casualty onto a stretcher as the ambulance arrived. We headed back to the station, congratulating each other on the job and I felt the beautiful taste of pride.

The culture was very much of teamwork in the fire brigade, and I picked that up immediately. No man was alone, we were all in it together and cohesion was very natural for the team, who saw each other being as essential as the equipment we required to do our job. I needed that, probably more than I realised after always being part of a team at work — always being relied on and relying on others equally. A unit, no one in solidarity.

There were plenty of practical jokes and general piss-taking, which was always welcomed. We used to have a toy spider attached to string that we would dangle out of the window on an evening. Unsuspecting members of the public, usually people on a night out drinking, would walk past and get a massive fright. We found it really amusing, childishly chuckling behind the glass. Until one night, a woman got such a shock that she ran into the road, narrowly missing an oncoming bus. After that, we stopped the spider practical joke in favour for others.

Another part of the culture of our station would be eating together. On a night shift, it would be around 8:30 pm and we would all have supper before going off to study or rest in the dorms. In the mornings, we would often have a game of tuggy, chasing each other around like schoolkids. The incoming shift would laugh and shake their heads, but it was great craic and these things kept us bonded.

Kind of like a family. But for all the jokes and messing around, there was never much rest as the police station was close by and the city centre location brought almost non-stop jobs.

In the autumn of my first year in the fire service, the Meadow Well riots happened. It was September 1991 and the riots caused mass destruction that took years to rebuild, leaving a scar on the area that is still talked about today, over three decades later.

The riots kicked off after a joyriding incident, but there had been increasing tension for years before this occurred between the residents and the police. The trigger incident in early September 1991 came from a police chase involving a stolen car. During the chase, the vehicle that the police were following crashed, killing the two passengers.

There had previously been anti-social behaviour in the area and a subsequent increase in police presence which had caused animosity. After the joyriding incident and deaths of the two young lads in the car, years of poverty, neglect, stigma, and tension erupted and a crescendo of rebellion began from the community as the riots broke out, lasting several days.

The irony was that the once close-knit community began attacking their own by looting the local shops and setting them on fire along with a community centre and medical centre. An electricity substation was burned out, leaving the estate in darkness through the night, the only light coming from petrol bombs and burning buildings.

Cars were stolen and burnt out. Chaos in the streets, from the locals against locals. They weren't angry with their neighbours; it was the police and politics that they perceived to be the problem. Local police would respond to the incidents only to be attacked – bricks thrown in their direction, petrol bombs launched, and traps in cul-de-sacs so offenders could target the emergency services.

The fire brigade had a heavy role to play, trying to control the many fires that were set throughout the day and night. All areas were called in and I remember going to the printer for the job, reading "civil disturbance in North Shields." We all got ready, and being from the area, I knew exactly where we were going, no A-Z map was needed.

On arrival, it was carnage. Hundreds and hundreds of people throwing petrol bombs, torching buildings and cars, looting the shops, bricks being launched at the police. It was utter madness, disturbing, and extremely sad. I had mixed emotions; home was only a ten-minute walk from the epicentre of the disruption. It was my stomping ground, I knew the people, the families.

It felt like an axe to my heart to see my area like this. A mass of devastation and angry people, feeling let down by society, but expressing it violently, impacting many, a ripple effect of chaos. On my doorstep, my home. I was gutted. But I wasn't there as a local resident. I was there as a firefighter, my duty in that moment was to help control the mayhem, keep people safe, and prevent further risk.

We entered shops, putting out the fires set by the residents and as we were going in, people were coming out covered in smoke, arms ladened with crates of beer, bottles of alcohol, nappies, anything they could get their hands on. Looting from their own community. Dogs were barking all around, residents were getting too close, approaching, and asking what was going on.

People were cheering and shouting, others throwing bottles and bricks — violence all around. It was surreal and I had to take a few deep breaths and focus on why I was there as I witnessed my community crumble. I knew dozens of the offenders, but they didn't know it was me with my breathing apparatus on. It wasn't until we had to change apparatus that I was spotted.

It wasn't hostile, we weren't the enemy, the police were. There was no vendetta against us for the most part, but we were still the authority. Bricks were aimed at the fire engine but once I was recognised by some, it ceased slightly, re-targeted at the police. After a few days, the East End of Newcastle and the West End of Newcastle also began rioting in response, spiralling out of control.

The Meadow Well riots were total carnage and devastation for residents, which has dogged the estate since. The recovery took years and cost millions. Houses, public services, and council buildings all needed repairing. Road barriers were built as a future prevention tactic, an increase in police patrols for months and years after.

Community cohesion had also eroded and needed to be rebuilt alongside the buildings that had been destroyed. Residents who had lived there all their lives wanted to move, leaving behind empty homes and derelict buildings. It was madness and it left the community with scars, but I learnt so much in those few weeks as a new firefighter, despite it feeling a tiny bit like my time in Northern Ireland.

Work continued to go well and ticked all the boxes in what I wanted for a job. The team were great, supporting one another and achieving our goals. The jobs were varied, and we knew we were helping people in their time of need. It was hard graft, but I loved it and felt I had a purpose that was more than just a job.

In December 1992, Carol and I got married. We buggered off to Florida, wanting no fuss. We both felt if we got married at home, it would be difficult to decide who to invite or find a venue big enough for all the people we had both met throughout our lives. So, we decided to go abroad and Orlando it was. We arrived in Florida and sought out a preacher, who advised us of the process we need to follow before the ceremony. A document had to be obtained from the County Court, before visiting the preacher and ensuring we had a witness.

A stunning venue was chosen – a lake with a lovely bridge and memorable views. There we met the preacher and his wife, who was to be the witness to our marriage. In retrospect, we arrived at a lake in the middle of nowhere and the preacher could have been a mass murderer, but along we trotted, me in my shorts and Carol in a dress that wasn't a traditional wedding dress, but still beautiful, and we got married. Just like that!

Even with a little knot of nerves in my stomach, it was a relaxed ceremony and Carol and me could have been the only people in the world during those 30 minutes, as we officially signed our commitment of love. I'd struck gold and felt the six-foot tall I would never be as we went to celebrate at a local water park. It was perfect and suited us just fine – in love and happy to be married, regardless of how and where.

As imagined, my mam wasn't best pleased when we returned as a married couple, getting hitched on the sly. However, she loved Carol and quickly accepted our choice when we all began celebrating. I'm not sure if she ever fully forgave me for sneaking off to get married, but at least she had my siblings whose wedding she could attend.

Everyone else was also quite narked that we buggered off to get married: Dad, my sister, and brothers, Carol's family and all our mates. But we made up for it with multiple celebrations and at the end of the day, we did what was right for us, which is the way a wedding should be.

Another big job came the following year, 1993. As usual, the station printer went off and I collected the job. The job was a factory fire on Norham Road, North Shields. The building was Ronson's – a lighter factory, and as we travelled in the engine along the Coast Road, we could see it glowing ferociously in the distance. A mass eruption of flames. The closer we got, the more devastating it looked.

The area was on a large plot of land, surrounded by other factories and businesses, with residential areas not far away. As we arrived at the site, because of the nature of the factory, there were small gas canisters for lighters that were exploding and raining down on us like cluster bombs. The roof was ablaze, and it was clear that the priority was to stop the fire spreading to the surrounding businesses.

There was a car showroom next door to the blaze, so some of us went to find the car keys from the showroom office to drive the cars away, or there would be further explosions. Eventually locating the keys to each car, like a frantic game of The Crystal Maze, we were off, like The Sweeney, speeding those cars away from the encroaching flames. Factories around Ronson's were destroyed, including a carpet factory as we battled the blaze all night before being relieved by the next team.

Shifts came and went with a mixture of jobs. Then in 1993 an incident happened that shocked the community, and my friendship circle. One evening, Carol and I were at home in North Shields, and there was a massive explosion during the night. Everyone woke and wondered what was going on as emergency services circled the area. The next morning on the news, there was coverage of an explosion at a local oil terminal.

Going to work that day, there were discussions about the blast, and it was mentioned that it could have been a bomb. A few days later, the explosion was suspected to be terrorism. It shocked and frightened the community, who naturally became worried about their own safety.

During this period, I used to play Sunday morning football with a local team and after the game, we would go to a nearby pub, The Queen's, to celebrate or commiserate. One of the lads who played on the team, Sean, was missing that Sunday – no alarm bells rang as people were often away working or with family.

As we sat in The Queen's, talking about the game, having a few laughs and supping our beers, the police came in and began taking photos down from the walls – photos of us all from the Sunday league, featuring Sean. We asked what was going on, faces twisted in confusion. It transpired that Sean McNulty, a local lad, had been arrested as an IRA bomber for carrying out the North Shields attack and another bombing in Gateshead. We were flabbergasted and it gave a sharp reality check that you just don't know people. Subsequently, Sean was sentenced to 25 years in jail in 1994 but was released as part of the Good Friday agreement in 2000.

The months rolled by, and I continued enjoying my job at Pilgrim Street. The team were a fantastic bunch, and I had the best of both worlds: an amazing job and being able to go home after work, surrounded by family, friends, and of course, Carol. Life was great.

I gained a lot of experience in the busy station with almost constant, diverse jobs. House fires, incidents at pubs, RTAs, and visiting services to carry out fire safety checks. We would also join other stations locally if they needed extra support. Always kept busy, and we were able to respond to the needs of the local area and residents. Job to job, with the community often coming out to give us food and drinks after jobs. People were grateful and kind. I loved those first few months at Pilgrim Street, the teamwork glowed more than any fire and I knew that this would be a career I could see myself in for a long time.

CHAPTER 19
CHLOE

Work and life outside of my employment continued in happy synchronicity. Carol and I had been talking about starting a family and decided it was the right time to try. I was in my late 20s by now, and Carol was a few years younger. She was still working at Newcastle Building Society, which she enjoyed, and we were settled. It felt like perfect time to expand our family, something we'd always had in mind as our relationship developed in the early days.

We soon got pregnant and were both buzzing. Norman had already become a father, with his wife Sandra – their daughter, Sally, was two years old. It was brilliant being an uncle and Norman was a great Dad, so I couldn't wait to extend our family and was bursting with love for my daughter before she was even born.

Friends around us were also having babies and growing their families. It was heartwarming to see my childhood mates all settled. We shared life together: the milestones, the challenges, the achievements, the celebrations, and commiserations.

By the time Carol and me were pregnant, Dave and his wife, Christine, had a boy called David and a daughter, Rachel. And John and his wife, Eva, also had children, a son, John and two daughters, Melissa and Nicola.

Whilst Carol was pregnant, we moved from our flat into a house just around the corner. With Carol working at the building society, she was able to help sort our mortgage, and after selling the flat we moved to a more spacious property that would become our family home – a place to make memories, the three of us.

I felt like I'd scored the winning goal, knowing we would be adding to our team with a little Stephenson. We enjoyed the build-up for our baby's arrival, despite the stress of moving house. Carol managed pregnancy well, she was blooming and we couldn't wait to be parents.

As it got closer to the baby's due date, I updated my gaffer. He advised that if Carol went into labour during a shift, I should be okay to leave unless there was a severe emergency. Sod's Law dictated that I was on shift when I received the call from Carol that she had gone into labour. It came in through the payphone at the station as we had no mobile phones back then, and luckily, I wasn't out at a job. Carol was packed, ready to go and would be heading to Rake Lane Hospital in North Tyneside. I was able to leave the site and was there at the birth of our baby daughter.

Chloe arrived in the world, the day after my 30th birthday, in February 1994. It was life-defining, life-affirming, love at first sight and all the other cliches people use – they are true! Here she was, a belated birthday present, all 6lbs 4oz of the beautiful tiny human that we had created and we both knew life would never be the same again, for all the right reasons.

I kissed my daughter's tiny head and looked into her perfect, scrunched-up face as I told her how incredible she was. I smiled at Carol, our world would change forever, now it would always be her, our number one. My heart was full, I had a wonderful wife, who would be an amazing mother, and the most perfect baby daughter who I promised I would love until my dying day.

Life did indeed alter, as it does for every parent, but I loved it. The enormity of the responsibility of parenthood was overwhelming but something I reflected on and embraced. My attitude and outlook changed in so many ways and I developed a personal new fear at work, one that I didn't have before.

My duty as a firefighter was always so strong, but I began to process my thinking and actions differently. I had another duty now, that of being a parent, and this tiny little human relied on me and her mam – we had to be our best. It was essential to me that I was a hands-on dad.

I hadn't experienced tactile affection from my own dad. Just like many men of his era, he didn't show his emotions and it cascaded down to no cuddles and not many words of love to us. I knew that I was loved, undoubtedly, but I wanted my child and any future children to feel that love in some of the ways I didn't.

I also wanted to be hands-on with looking after the baby, and Carol's employment and my work meant that was possible. I was able to experience time with her, just Chloe and me, which was precious. Seeing my baby grow and develop, her personality evolving, it was a gift. I would watch her for hours, mesmerised by this incredible, tiny human, witnessing changes in her as my heart swelled.

Carol loved being a mother, it suited her, and she made the hard work of child-rearing look easy with her naturally caring personality. We were a great team and life was amazing, the three of us, surrounded by family and friends. Chloe was a bundle of love and everyone around her absorbed her sparkle.

We were lucky enough to have family around us for support: Carol's mam, my parents, and siblings. Mam was an immense help from the start. After Carol went back to work, I would care for Chloe around my shift patterns. When Carol and I were both at work, my mam would babysit Chloe, a pleasure for her as Grandma and important for Chloe. Then after a shift at work, I would rush home, desperate to see Chloe – she was my everything.

When I had days off from my rota and around my shifts, I would take Chloe to the park, the beach, and the library. She was a little joy, and I treasured our time together. I began taking her to playgroups as she developed. It was much less of a thing in the 90s — dads taking their babies to groups solo, but I loved it. I think I got as much out of it as Chloe, hearing all the mams talk about their babies' development, this and that, tips and hints at different ages, alongside seeing Chloe interact with the other babies. I felt accepted and part of the group, despite my gender. The detail of the breastfeeding and cracked nipples was a bit too much for me though!

At times it was surreal – a few hours earlier I could have been cutting a person out of a car or dragging a casualty out of a burning building. I could never have seen myself attending playgroups when I was a newly qualified Marine, it just wasn't on my radar, but I wouldn't have changed it for the world.

After I had a day with Chloe, Carol would return home from work and do the evening routine, bathing Chloe, singing, and reading to her – having her own important, precious time with the baby. At the weekends, it was family time and the three of us would go out for the day, or visit family and friends.

Living close to my parents, Mam, in particular, was always a great help. She loved being a grandma and it was support for us as new parents. Mam already supported Norman and Sandra with Sally and I know that my mam was a big influence on my kids, the way she showed them love, it was great for me to see and I'm thankful both my children were able to have such a strong relationship with Mam and Dad.

Chloe's personality began to develop. She was a tough little cookie, and nothing was a bother to her. Alongside this, she was fiercely independent and determined — she still is to this day. She was a slow starter to walk, taking her first steps on holiday around the swimming pool. After that, she couldn't stop, and we would be on alert as her curiosity and mobility grew.

We had an awful incident when she was a toddler. It was a Saturday and Carol and I had taken her out to the local shopping centre. Walking from shop to shop, Chloe tripped up and smashed her head on the side of a wooden bench. Her forehead burst open and blood was gushing from just above her eye. It was a gaping wound and we both felt our hearts almost stop as we saw our cherished baby screaming and covered in blood. I tried to stay calm, as I felt a fear that I had never experienced in my life pressing tightly around my neck.

Carol rushed into a shop to ring an ambulance as I scooped up our tiny daughter and held her in my arms, one hand pressing on the open wound, trying to soothe her as she screamed louder than the sirens that would soon reach us. She was hysterical, her little face covered in blood and tears, as I looked at my precious baby, willing the ambulance to arrive.

When it did reach us and we subsequently arrived at A&E, we were advised the injury was so bad that we had to transfer to the specialist unit at another hospital for plastic surgery. Panic saturated us as parents. We eventually got to the RVI hospital, nerves shot, and Chloe's wound was stitched. She had to remain in hospital for recovery and a few hours later, although not quite herself, she was happily chatting in her hospital bed, bouncing back in the way she continued to do as she grew up.

All I could hear every now and then were collective chants and noises faintly in the background. My beloved Newcastle United were playing football less than a mile away in St. James's Park where I should have been with my season ticket — and instead, I was sat in hospital, hearing cheers and boos, desperate to know what was happening. But my world was in front of me — our wounded mini-soldier, and my wife. My first love of football was most definitely on the bench now my family had arrived!

CHAPTER 20
TOO CLOSE FOR COMFORT

In 1995 there was a large explosion on the river at AMEC, an offshore manufacturing company. I was on shift when the job came in and the crew reacted the same way we always did, calmly and promptly getting mobilised. As much as it was now my natural routine, getting ready for this particular job was accompanied by frantic terror.

The job sheet stated persons reported and due to the sound of the job and the nature of the surroundings, there were likely to be significant injuries and fatalities. Horrendous in any job but this job was personal for me, and I felt bile rise in my throat as I got ready to attend with my crew. My best mate Dave worked at AMEC, and I knew he was on shift that day.

Our crew travelled to the location, I was quieter than my usual self, my stomach doing somersaults and my heart rate increasing as we approached the site. All I could think of was that Dave could be involved – that my mate could be hurt or worse. Pulling up in the emergency tender, two engines from the nearest station, Wallsend, had arrived at the scene.

My gaffer and me liaised with the Wallsend crew when we disembarked the vehicle. They advised us it was a bad job and asked if we had body bags on board – which we did. I thought I was going to pass out as panic spread through me like an ink blot on a page. We reached the rig where the devastation had happened via a gangplank.

AMEC had hundreds of people working at the site and a busy shift pattern. I tried to focus on why I was there, my duty, rather than the overwhelming dizziness threatening to take me out. On our approach to the entrance, we could see the faces of our Wallsend colleagues, demonstrating the horror of what they had witnessed. The explosion had been contained and the destruction was visible. The blast killed two men instantly, injuring another who subsequently died.

The area was eerily quiet, and we had to search for and retrieve the bodies. All I remember thinking was that I had to know if one of the fatalities was Dave but at the same time, God, I really didn't want to know. My mind was drowning in anxiety while we located the bodies of these poor victims. My mouth dry, I looked, and was relieved to know it wasn't Dave. I immediately felt the sledgehammer of sadness. Those men were someone else's best friend, someone's son, dad, and husband.

It was a horrendous day and a tragedy that impacted many. One of the lads at Wallsend station actually left the job following the AMEC incident as he was so traumatised. For all we tried to help people and respond to emergencies, much of the time images could never be erased from our mind. It takes its toll and for some, it would become the final bit of scaffolding keeping that worker up — once it's taken away, they can't do it anymore. We all have our limits and alongside the highs of the rescues, were the catastrophic lows that everyone felt in their own way.

The mind can be a haunting machine and in those days we didn't have the professional support to decompress from a job. There was no expert to talk to about the reoccurring nightmares and flashbacks in our head from what we had witnessed and what had been burnt into our minds forever. Added to this, the men across the service didn't talk about how they felt with one another. No discussions of struggling, fear, and the poisonous thought of thinking you could have done more – if only you had done something else. Instead, we used the only thing we could to help get through the trauma, smiles, banter, and respect.

It was often job after job, boom, boom, boom, with no time to absorb what we may have seen and reflect – until you were in the shower at home, in a trance of what the fuck? Men were told to "man up," and they still are, although now to a lesser degree. That was the narrative, in work, in society, in the world. We all knew what the job was about, of course we did. But we were all human and the job impacted each of us differently. Like in any other profession, we had colleagues having breakdowns and becoming mentally unwell across the service.

My family helped me to switch off, but it wasn't always easy and if I ever stopped thinking about the tragedy or became complacent to it, I knew it would be the day that I would no longer be right for the fire service. As well as family responsibilities, I had other ways of keeping well; ones I had used since I was a kid and from when I joined the Royal Marines. Exercise, trying to stay positive and having a focused mindset, as well as trying to use humour – but all of these had their limits at times and sometimes the funny man couldn't laugh anymore.

Luckily, our crew were phenomenal and right from the start, I clicked with them. Many of the lads were older and there was one younger lad, Niall. We hit it off immediately. New lads and gaffers joined and were instantly accepted into the work family such as Squish, Davey, and Phil, good blokes who will always be friends. We were a social watch, with regular nights out for a few beers and a continued effort to bond, support, and look after each other in the way lads do.

Shifts rolled into shifts as time passed at a speed we were all astonished by. Jobs continued and it was seldom quiet. Another memorable incident occurred at a block of flats around the corner from the station. The job came in — a flat fire — and we all got to action. On arrival, there was no sign on the outside of a fire. We entered the block of flats and spoke to the concierge who was drunk and gave us no indication of where the fire was. One of our colleagues came into the foyer and told us that a man was hanging out of the window and smoke was coming from that window.

The flat was on the seventh floor and this poor bloke was clinging on for dear life. Up we rushed with our equipment. Myself and a bloke called Duncan went to the fourth floor via the lift. You never get out of the lift on the floor the fire is on as it could result in walking into the flames. Instead, we worked our way up the stairs, carrying all the equipment – hammers, hose, enforcers, and breathing apparatus — as we moved quickly up the floors.

Arriving at the flat, the door was locked, and smoke billowed out from under the door. Duncan, who was a 6'2" brick shithouse grabbed the sledgehammer and began pounding the door with it. I sat on the floor, in between his legs and kicked against the front door, both desperately attempting to get into the flat to rescue the bloke hanging from his fingernails on the window ledge outside.

Eventually, the door gave way, and we were confronted with the blazing fire. We began extinguishing the flames promptly, shouting reassuringly to the guy that we were almost there. Then as we went to help the resident, only a metre or so away, he dropped from the window ledge to the ground outside the block of flats.

Duncan and I looked at one another, reading each other's minds and said,

'SHIT!' in unison, rushing to the window.

The fire service doesn't have anything to collect people falling from buildings — no blankets, trampolines, or massive fishing nets — that only happens in the films! Luckily for our guy, there was a flat roof attached to the building with bin storage underneath. He had landed on this roof and was unconscious. A turntable ladder was then sent up to rescue the man. Eventually, they reached him and began first aid. He was still alive and was transported to the hospital, where he survived, despite life-changing injuries.

The man ended up being part of a BBC documentary about his near-death experience. It was a relief the bloke survived but I was fuming with the concierge and even went looking for him, full of rage and with words running through my head that I wanted to say. Ultimately, his misconduct cost us time which could have prevented the injuries of the resident as well as putting everyone else at risk.

As time went on in the fire service and new lads joined, I was no longer the proby. Along with other team members, I would mentor the recruits, always great lads who fit well into the team, our work family.

Another memorable job that is still etched in my brain came in one shift. The job read "man with a Lucozade bottle stuck on his penis, handcuffed to a bed." Shaking my head, all I could think was for fuck's sake! As a service, we would sometimes get paramedics calling us to assist in incidents involving people being "stuck" and this was one of those times. As we drove to the location, I said to the gaffer that I couldn't go into the job. I kindly asked,

'Boss, is there any chance I can pass on this one, please? I don't want to go in.'

It was likely that I sounded like a whiny teenager and he looked and me, flatly telling me to shut up and get in. But I just couldn't face it. There were quite a few of us that turned up to the job, so I knew the unfortunate man would get relief! But I just couldn't handle it and didn't know if I could remain professional in a job like that.

Not only was it way out of my comfort zone and probably many of the lad's comfort zones, but I didn't want to laugh as it was likely the man would already be embarrassed and in pain. I also knew I would struggle to demonstrate empathy in a situation like that, which is always needed to help people in their time of need – even those with bizarre sexual fetishes.

So, there I was arguing with the boss, keeping eye contact, and telling him I would take a written warning if I had to, whilst my colleagues were sniggering. Luckily, the emergency tender arrived with some more lads who would do the job. After all, they had the specialist equipment on board for getting a bloke's dick out of a bottle — which in this instance included taking a hammer to the said bottle and freeing the man's genitals.

When we got back to the station, the gaffer gave me a bollocking for not dealing with the bollocks. He was right, but I had my limits, and the job wasn't life-threatening. If it had been then I absolutely would have dealt with it, bollocks and all. Everyone laughed about it, humour was necessary in the fire service, and no one ever forgot the bloke who was attracted to that Lucozade bottle!

CHAPTER 21
JAKE

Jake arrived in the world in September 1996. By this time, Chloe was just over two years old. She was a proud big sister from the start and still is. Like Chloe, baby number two was planned, and Carol bloomed in pregnancy once again. It was harder for us both already having Chloe, but when Jake was born, our family was complete, and my heart was full to have both a daughter and a son.

I had so much love to give my two children and being a dad was the best gift that life could give me. I was thankful each day for my blessings. Jake completed my dream, our bonny lad who I hoped I could pass on all the important things in life, just like I would to Chloe.

As Jake joined the Stephenson clan, his arrival added to the bond my sibling's children all had. Each of the kids in our family are around two years apart in age; Sally, Chloe, Jake, Abbie, and Alex. Jake is the only boy and like with Chloe, I was at the birth, getting more involved this time as Carol did the hard work. Our little lad was born a perfect bundle of 7lb 2oz's of joy. Life adapted into another routine as we managed a toddler and a newborn.

It took some readjusting, especially after getting in from a night shift, but it was magical, and our family was perfect. Carol still worked at Newcastle Building Society in the city centre, and I remained at Delta Green. She would get ready for work, organise the kids and bring them up in the car to the fire station, where we would do the handover for me finishing my shift and returning home.

It was nice for the lads on shift to see my kids and as Chloe and Jake grew older, they enjoyed looking around the fire station and meeting my work family. Perhaps that gave them a taste for the career themselves from such an early age as they both now work for Tyne and Wear Fire and Rescue Service, as does my niece, Abbie.

Fatherhood was my most cherished role, the duty that would always be my number one priority. Most lads, when younger, don't think about becoming a dad and for me, my career was always the focus – well that and football and socialising with the lads! My family and my love for the kids felt as essential as breathing. They were part of my functioning and everything I did from the moment I became a father was for my children. Every action, every decision, they were at the centre – and still are.

By the time Jake was going to the same playgroups that I had taken Chloe to three years earlier, she was attending nursery. Jake and I would drop Chloe off for her morning at nursery — after getting her ready and me styling her hair up like an apparent pineapple (that she still goes on about today). She would happily skip into nursery as I waved goodbye, and then Jake and me would go to the local playgroup.

By this time, I was a dab hand at the groups. I had learnt so much when Chloe was a baby and was older myself, being in my early 30s. With age and experience came a confidence in my abilities to be the best dad I could.

It was great to see Jake interacting and to witness the subtle differences in the personalities of my kids at that age. He was fascinating and I would watch him, a smile plastered on my face, as he began to make sense of the world in his own way. Tiny experiences, expressions, and actions that I'd never forget, woven into the tapestry of our family story. It was priceless and a time I'm so thankful for, knowing not all dad's get that opportunity.

I was grateful to have the quality time with Jake that I had experienced with Chloe when she was a baby, fitting it around my shifts in the fire service. Jake was the opposite of Chloe in many ways, their personalities varied, and the gender differences were apparent. Jake was into everything, even as a baby and was a lot more demanding (in a nice way).

He would make me laugh with his little ways, my jaw aching after a few hours out and about with him and he was always making a noise — I was pleased I was an experienced dad and on the ball. Jake couldn't be put down for a second as he would be off looking for bother. If I glanced away, he was gone, like magic. He was loud, fast, and cheeky – probably much like his dad as a baby.

We would do things at weekends as a family such as visits to the park or beach. Chloe hated sand and still does. We would place her on a towel, and she would just sit there, content playing and looking around. Not Jake. He would be off, full of energy and a need to explore. A little bugger who was full of adventure!

Carol continued to be an amazing mother, balancing her different roles, working hard then coming home and seeing to the kids each evening, having her precious time with them. She would return from work and if it had been a stressful day for me with the kids, I would go out for a run – my own tonic to keeping myself sane and the way I have always been able to reflect and refocus. The kids got the best of both worlds; me through the day, then time with their mam and me on the evenings and weekends. We were happy, grateful, and had a home filled with love.

As soon as Jake could walk, we were kicking a ball. I knew he would adore football; he was my bairn after all, but I wanted to make sure. We would spend hours in the garden, playing football, laughing, and making memories, along with probably pissing the neighbours off with the noise. I would watch him kicking the ball on the grass, his co-ordination developing, and he would look back at me, a wide smile on his face as I clapped my hands and cheered him on. Each season I would get him the latest Newcastle United team strip and we would spend hours talking about our beloved team and the players, his eyes wide, completely engaged in the discussion.

Shifts at Delta Green could be challenging, just as they had been from day one. After work, I often couldn't dwell on some of the horrors, near misses, and fatalities I had seen during a shift. I knew when I got home, I would be straight into Dad mode. It was hard but I would try and get five minutes to decompress at the end of a shift, focusing my mindset away from work and onto the kids.

It was a relief in many ways to almost be forced to turn that work switch off – I'm certain on numerous occasions it stopped me ruminating and helped me process some of the traumatic situations I found myself in. But it wasn't without challenge. My family was my support. The gift of my two children and wife could make the hardest of shifts easier, my gratitude for having what people could never have or had lost.

Sometimes even knowing I had to get back and make sure we had nappies and a picnic packed for the day was the best therapy after a challenging shift. They helped my mindset in so many ways. From the day Chloe, and subsequently, Jake, were born, my duty as a father became the most important thing in my life.

Mam continued to be a great help and so did Dad. It was nice, but also strange to see the relationship he had with my kids compared to how he was with us when we were kids. Dad was so much more tactile and relaxed with his grandkids, perhaps he mellowed in old age. It was lovely and both Chloe and Jake developed amazing relationships with their grandparents, which I'm forever thankful for.

It was soon time for Jake to begin school, attending the same junior school as Chloe. This also meant that I had a bit more time to myself when I wasn't at work. I remember one time running down the coast and seeing the Newcastle United team doing a pre-season training session on the beach. Players such as Shola Ameobi, Kieron Dyer, and Robbie Elliott were kicking the ball, practising their skill with ease. I watched them for a minute or so, mesmerised by their form and buzzing to be able to witness my favourite sport on my favourite beach.

I thought about how much Jake would love to see his team on his local beach. Clapping my hands together I thought *fuck it* and dashed to the school. When I arrived, I told reception I need to collect Jake Stephenson as he had a dentist appointment. After being directed to his classroom, in I went and repeated the message to his teacher, Mrs Pallen, glancing at Jake. His little face looked back, brow furrowed, as I told him to hurry up and get his bag. He followed orders, scratching his head as I rushed him out of the classroom. As soon as we got out of the room, I turned to him and said,

'Howay Jakey, the Toon are at the beach!'

We rushed back to the beach and the players were still there. Jake sat in awe, mouth open, watching his beloved team like it was the best thing in the whole wide world. The look on his face was priceless and for me, a precious memory that was more important than a maths lesson.

CHAPTER 22
A NEW CENTURY

It was the last few days of 1999, before the Millennium arrived. I would have preferred to be with my family at home as the new century began, but the next best thing was to be with my work family. Being in a city centre station, life was always buzzing but the Millennium was something special.

Just before midnight, everyone on shift headed up to the roof of the station. From there, you could see for miles, all the lights across the city, sparkling like gems on the most beautiful necklace. It was magical and as the new century started, we stood in silent reflection. I looked around, staring into the city and thinking about my own life as we all took a moment to appreciate one another, our jobs, our city, our health, and the love of our families. We were the lucky ones.

The Millennium turned and time went on, then the world received a life-altering shock in September 2001 with the 9/11 terrorist attacks in New York City. Something we all remember and a devastation the world felt. At the time, I was at work, chatting in the canteen.

The news came on, interrupting some programme that was playing as background noise to us lads talking and laughing. A blanket of silence swallowed our voices as we all fixed our eyes on the horror being broadcast. I'm sure we all felt our hearts stop for a moment as we watched, eyes wide. The carnage of the terrorist attack unfolded on our TV screen, the crew staring, hands to mouths and heads shaking in disbelief.

As firefighters, we had an empathetic point of view with our colleagues in New York who were embarking on a rescue mission to try and save people from the aftermath of the heartbreaking attack. We could see the fear on their faces and could almost feel the desperate anxiety, diluted by the duty they carried as they went into those buildings, knowing that they were unlikely to come out alive.

The devastation proved us right and our colleagues in America were amongst over 2,500 people who tragically lost their lives that day. That's not to mention the fatalities in the days after, and years later from physical health damage – never mind the psychological impact. So many deaths and a ripple effect of tragedy and sadness that still haunts people over 20 years later. Hate, harm, heartbreak.

During that shift, we received a memo from HQ telling us to be on high alert — after all, this wasn't expected anywhere in the world and could therefore happen anywhere. It was a sobering day and the days that followed were a period of silent reflection. Cruel, targeted attacks and the loss of so many people undoubtedly make you think of your own mortality. We had always been lucky, never losing anyone in the line of duty, but it didn't mean it couldn't happen. Nor were we immune from the warped, sadistic minds of terrorists and criminals. Our hearts went out to all, the bravery and loss of so many victims of those attacks and subsequent attacks, including our brothers, the firefighters.

Risk was a hard thing to digest in the fire service. We were skilled, trained officers and had the latest firefighting equipment at the time, but there was always a call between taking the risk or not – and some of us, despite training, had the inclination to push the boundaries of safety from our own ethical point and values. Our gaffers always kept us right, being the voice of experience, but it could be challenging at times and no two situations were ever the same. Often, you were alone or only with another firefighter and had to make that judgement call in a split second.

An example of this came into practice during a job involving a house fire in Gateshead. Not our usual area, but the team in Gateshead was busy so as a crew, we helped out. Off we went and on arrival in the street, a property was ablaze. Neighbours were outside, pacing the pavement as they watched the inferno. Asking if there was anyone in the property, we were advised by anxious neighbours that an elderly woman lived there.

The gaffer gave orders, and me and another lad entered the property. We began putting the fire out. I travelled up the stairs, controlling the fire and searching for casualties. I located a body in a bedroom on a bed. Looking at the scene, I made an assessment and decision to leave the body there, due to significant burning.

I radioed my colleague outside to advise that I had located the body and would be leaving it there, rather than bringing it outside. The colleague on the other end of the radio questioned my decision as it's not normal to leave a body unless categorically sure they are deceased from your risk assessment and checks. My gaffer came on the radio to confirm I was sure that the person was deceased.

I had a decision to make for forensic reasons also – a potential crime scene. It was a huge decision to leave the woman, feeling almost unnatural. So many times we had pulled bodies from fires to work on them. But here, the woman was unfortunately dead, and her body had begun melting into the furniture. It was a tragic site and I believe it was caused by the elderly woman smoking in bed. We couldn't always get the outcomes we wanted at work, it was the sad reality, and death was common.

On shift, the watch often got called to assist with possible jumpers from the Tyne Bridge. Unfortunately, it was and still is, a common spot for people in desperate emotional distress. We would be asked to help as a "silent approach," with no blue lights that could add to the concern. Police would be at the scene, usually with the police negotiator trying to talk the person down from the bridge to a place of safety, and we would be situated at the Quayside, just under the bridge.

One time we arrived at the Quayside at 2:00 am and saw a woman halfway on the parapet over the bridge. The police were talking to her, and we assumed they would be getting her back over the right side of the bridge within minutes by our first impressions of the scenario. As we waited, ready to help if needed, we were soon distracted and my colleague, Dave and I began talking about the weekend and perhaps going for a few pints. Nodding and smiling, the conversation progressed about where we could start the night and we began to plan a pub crawl route that was abruptly interrupted by a massive splash and a,

'FUCK,' from us both as we jumped out of the vehicle and grabbed the rope to try and assist with the rescue of the jumper.

The Foxtrot rescue boat was waiting and thankfully saved the lady. Sadly, jumpers weren't always rescued, or they died in the water before they could be reached, which I would find out in a future role.

As time progressed, more lads joined the crew – Den, Mel, and Sticks. One night on shift we were all in the communal lounge, along with a lad who was detached, offering temporary support as we were short-staffed. I was bang into my fitness, as I always had been and at the time, abs belts were all the rage. Basically, you would wrap these wide, support-style belts around your stomach, securing them with strips of Velcro. Electrodes travelled through the belt on a current, in an attempt to stimulate the muscles and allegedly help produce a six-pack. Of course, I was certain it was all bullshit, but I had one of the belts and after talking about it with the lads, it led to four or five of them also purchasing one.

One night we were all sat there on our break, ab belts around our guts of different sizes, watching *Match of the Day* with a chorus of noises and sharp body movements from us as our ab belts did their supposed work. The lad on detachment was a real bore and we were sitting, rolling our eyes, and bitching about how dull he was.

As the banter went on, people started exiting the room and we realised the boring lad was in the room. Colleagues were getting up and leaving and it transpired that a post-it note had been getting passed around telling us all to shut the fuck up as the target of our piss-taking was at the back of the room! They didn't bother passing it to me and instead made me look like a right bastard. Of course, it was all banter and I apologised to the lad after, who took it in good humour.

Another couple of probies joined the watch towards the end of my time in Delta Green; Casper and Jinxy. Casper's name was Scotty, but he got referred to as the friendly ghost as he was so pale. When Jinxy joined, I walked into the room and pretended to be the gaffer, giving him grief for sitting relaxing and talking to the crew. Shaking my head at him and keeping my voice steady and assertive, I kept it up for a good ten minutes, as the colour in his face turned an increasing brighter shade of red before I bent over laughing and gave him a handshake and welcome hug. When Jinxy joined, we had a massive spate of deaths in a small period of time. Not a shift went by without a fatality or serious incident, and that's how he got his nickname – he was most definitely a jinx.

We all tried to use banter in the crew, it was essential to keep us going and always brought us together. With all the devastation in the job, humour was our counselling, the way we digested some of the horrendous jobs, and the way we cared for one another. I'm certain the hundreds of laughs got each and every one of us through some of the traumatic jobs that haunted us as individuals.

During my time at Delta Green, Carol and me sadly split up. It was 2005 and there was no major incident and no one else was involved. We just drifted apart, and we were different people to what we'd been when we first met and fell in love — having children, growing up, these are all things that change you. We hadn't been getting on great and decided that we didn't want any deterioration to impact the kids, so we separated. It was an enormously difficult thing to do, a real kick in the stomach for what I thought would be my forever.

I left Carol and the kids in the family home and moved to a flat close by, a cloud of failure hanging over me that needed time to disperse. It was extremely hard telling the kids, who were both still young at almost 12 and 9 years old. They were devastated and it felt like a knife in my heart, but Carol and I talked to them about double the birthdays and double the Christmas's, trying to focus on the positives. Carol and I still loved one another as people, we just weren't in love anymore. We knew we could co-parent and still be friends, putting the kids first like we always had.

Chloe and Jake began spending half the week with me in my flat and the other half of the week with Carol at the family home. I can't say it was easy, it was a wound that took a long time to heal, and I felt lost for a while. My colleagues at work and my best mates, Dave and John, were very supportive and I will forever thank them for that – I really needed it during that period. But I knew it was the best decision for the kids, and Carol and I both acknowledged that.

Splitting up was also the right thing for Carol and me as people, but it didn't stop me from being absolutely gutted. I was almost 40 years old and the future I thought I had was no more. I used my reliable exercise as a coping mechanism and also made friends with a neighbour, Chris, who was a single dad to two kids after his wife tragically died.

It was hard managing the kids alone for half the week, but my parents were always happy to help. The kids were my world, they still are, so we all adapted, and life soon settled down into a new normal. By this time, both Chloe and Jake were well-formed kids and enjoyed school and had built good friendship groups.

Chloe was very clever, like her mam, and did well in all her studies. She was always enthusiastic to try sports, but it wasn't where her skill set lay! We still joke about it now. Luckily, she was exceptional academically but also found a sport for her which was cheerleading. It was gymnastic based, and she toured the country for a local team.

Jake was brilliant at sports. He joined the local football team at North Shields and was scouted by Newcastle and Sunderland, training at their academies. The kids continued to have a great relationship and Chloe would look out for her brother at school, even though he would insist he didn't need it – much of the time it would be her covert operation, wanting to protect. They were always close as kids and still are today.

Jake is very much like me in nature and was a bit of a chancer as a kid but nothing phased Chloe – she was forever calm and looked out for her little brother. As their home life changed, Chloe continued to be the little nurturer and they both settled into their new routine. Luckily, they also made friends with the neighbour's kids who were of a similar age and life went on, albeit a bit differently for everyone.

In 2005, we received a shock at work with the news that Delta Green was going to close. A strategic decision had been made to close our Pilgrim Street station and another nearby station due to costs. It was a blow we weren't expecting and a big deal for our close-knit crew. And it wasn't just Green watch who had a bond, all the lads across the other three shifts were spot on. As a collective, we were one big, brilliant watch. It would be the end of an era. And for me personally, a time when things were changing both in and outside of work.

CHAPTER 23
FOXTROT GREEN

It was the end of an era as life at Delta Green finished. We all had to think about where we would be moving on to and were offered some options. A new station was being built at the Fossway, Byker and it included a river rescue boat. I decided I wanted to go there, as did the bulk of my watch. It was called Foxtrot and we would be on Green watch. Foxtrot was a brand-new building, very different to the old station at Pilgrim Street and had private rooms, whereas we were used to a dorm at Pilgrim Street.

One morning before starting, I decided to go to the site and try and bag the best room. Sneaking in, I saw two other lads who had the same idea. We laughed at the cheek of us all, but each of us managed to get a decent room. There had been lots of change; a new station and the end of my marriage with Carol. But I was still grateful to have my amazing kids and support around me which included my sister, Julie, and her husband, Mark, who really helped out with Chloe and Jake.

When we started at Foxtrot, we had a new gaffer, Jock. He was a great boss, alongside Lee, the crew manager.

Some of us lads, Jinxy, Phil and others, met new blokes on the team including Paul, Martin, Roy, Badger, and Tommy. We all gelled, and it was important given the solid team we had come from. Naill from Pilgrim Street joined us later, along with Dunc and Paul, and with all our skills, we were able to be the best we could be as an experienced watch.

Foxtrot had a category one vehicle, a category two vehicle, and a turntable ladder, as well as being responsible for the river, meaning we had a fire boat. At the time it was an old, tired boat but as we started, a new speed boat arrived. It held six of us, lots of equipment and was the real deal, Miami Vice style, that we all learnt to use.

One of my first jobs at Foxtrot was a bin truck fire in Walker. The vehicle was driving around the streets of Walker and the driver, and his team were oblivious to it being on fire. So, there we were searching for a bin truck that was alight and on the move in the streets of Walker. We located the vehicle, and they were still in their own world until we reached the traffic lights and eventually communicated to the driver and passengers what was going on.

I soon had the opportunity to go out on the boat and it was something I really enjoyed. As time progressed, being the first responder team for any water incidents, we often received jobs for possible jumpers on the Tyne Bridge. We would wait in the dark, as to not cause more alarm and distress. One night, in the early hours, we were called to an incident. A jumper was on the bridge and as we waited in the boat, we got the call that he had gone into the river.

We travelled up with our searchlights on and spotted the person, face down in the river. Safely removing him from the water, he was unconscious, so we began performing first aid on him. Placing the oxygen on the casualty, myself and Tommy, half brought him around. We had a lamp that we had been using to find the casualty. As we continued to administer first aid, I said to Tommy,

'Pass that light over here.'

It was a huge light and as Tommy passed it, it dropped onto the casualty's head.

We began bickering about who had dropped it as I shouted,

'We've just fucking saved him, and you've fucking killed him.'

The gaffer screamed at us to shut the fuck up and like told-off school kids, we stopped bickering. Luckily, the jumper survived, despite concussion and a massive lump on his head from a falling lamp!

We were always informed about the outcome of the jumpers, if they survived or not, as it was part of our reporting procedures. It was sadly very common for people to go to the bridge, feeling suicidal. The death rate of those who jumped off the bridge was tragically high, and we would often be called to retrieve the body.

As the River Tyne is tidal, when the tide is out, there would be bodies uncovered. Very distressing for dog walkers or members of the public to discover, and unpleasant for us as the fire service having to remove bodies from the thick mud of the riverbanks in a respectful manner, retaining the person's dignity.

It's an awful thing, not exclusive to our city, and I hope that as services have developed and understanding about mental health has increased, people get support where possible. We helped to get the Samaritans signs placed on the Tyne Bridge and I hope these signs with helpline numbers have provided a deterrent over the years to people struggling so much that they feel it is the only way out.

Foxtrot was designated as the swift water rescue team, given our location and boat. The crew were to complete training in Bala, Wales, to advance our skills in water rescue. It was an excellent course and after finishing it, I was eager to get on with the job. It also meant we could help in different parts of the North East and beyond when incidents such as floods occurred, as well as to physically enter water when someone jumped off the bridge as we were now trained in swimming techniques and had new equipment to support rescue.

Being in the fire service highlighted many ways people struggle in life and we were often asked by the police and paramedics to assist with situations in people's own homes. An example was a call we received from paramedics requesting we help a morbidly obese man out of his bedroom in order to attend an appointment. The gaffer, Paul, Phil, and me went to the job. Reaching the property, we all went upstairs, where we saw a man who had been bed-bound for many years, almost confined to the small room.

The man was a bariatric patient and paramedics were struggling to assist him out of the bed and to the ambulance that was waiting to transport him to a hospital appointment. The guy lived with his mother and must have been in his late 30s or early 40s. It struck me as so sad that this was his life – bed-bound and never going out. Physical fitness had always been such a huge part of my world, but it didn't just keep my body healthy, it kept my mind focused, sharp, and well. I couldn't even begin to imagine the life this bloke had.

It's hard not to have escalating thoughts and judgements but I had empathy for his situation. I've learnt a lot about eating disorders in my later life through my fitness and business, and in many ways, obese people are judged and frowned upon whereas anorexic people tend to get a little more empathy. But it's all problem eating and poor body image, and people should be supported regardless.

Perhaps I was wrong and maybe he was happy with his life, but I very much doubted it; there was a sadness in the air. Along with this, there was an incredible stench of his body odour and bodily fluids. It was difficult not to gag but it also felt like a safeguarding issue and that no one should be living like that. Although I'm not sure it could really be called living — to me it felt like he was just existing.

We decided that the window couldn't come out, so we had to get the patient through the bedroom door. The paramedics brought their bariatric stretcher and we planned to manoeuvre him to the stretcher by transferring him as a team on a sheet. The man was naked, and we had to try and move him, whilst keeping his dignity.

It was one of those jobs where I thought a bit of banter could help, so I began having a chat with the guy, talking about football and general patter as we explained the plan to move him, hoping it would put him a little at ease. He seemed grateful for the communication and the clarity on what was no doubt an anxiety-provoking situation for him. We began the positioning, getting a sheet underneath him and placing the quilt over him to protect his modesty for when we got outside.

As we lifted the man, I had the gaffer on the side with me and Phil and Paul were on the opposite side. I looked across at Phil and gave him a wink. Then I glanced at Paul, who was in line with the bloke's arse as he lay on his side. We all had our share of holding the weight of the man and couldn't put him down, but I managed to move the quilt ever so slightly meaning that Paul got a face full of arse!

The guy didn't notice, instead, he was very grateful for our help but Paul, who was previously a kickboxer, gave me a look that could have landed him the lead role in a gangster film. The death stare bore into me as I pressed my lips together. He sneered across the blanket,

'Fucking hell, mate.'

I said a quick, insincere apology as the quilt was rearranged and we continued to get the man towards the ambulance. Eventually, he was safely in the ambulance and could attend his appointment at the hospital. Good work all round. Except as soon as the ambulance drove off, I had to sprint away almost as quickly as the ambulance took off, from the man mountain that was Paul and his promises to kill me.

Doing a runner down the street, shouting apologies in between pissing myself laughing, he chased me advising me I was dead when he got a hold of me. However, being little and lean, and having legs that could go as fast as the Warner Brothers cartoon character Road Runner, I had a head start! Luckily, Paul's anger dissolved, and he saw the funny side after a while.

The speed boat rescue came in useful once again when actor and presenter Robson Green was involved with his programme, Wild Swimming Adventure. Filming was happening on the River Tyne and we were there as a rescue boat in case needed, but Robson also wanted to advertise what we did as a service. We re-enacted what we would do in a real-life situation and ended up on the TV as part of the documentary — our little brush with a celebrity.

During my time working in Byker, my dad died. It was 2007 and Dad was typical of men of his generation in that he didn't go to the doctors. He was stubborn and always said he didn't want to put the doctor out, despite being nagged by us kids and Mam. Although he was getting older, we all noticed he wasn't as energetic as he had been and had lost weight.

By now, he was in his 70s and eventually, we persuaded him to go to the doctor. After some tests, Dad ended up in hospital. He was diagnosed with asbestosis and cancer and told he would only have a few months to live. It was devastating as we visited every day, watching him deteriorating before our eyes. Dad had always been strong and now he was vulnerable, frail, and disappearing in front of us.

I had planned a holiday; me and the kids along with my neighbour, Chris and his children. Mam told us to go and that Dad would still be here when we got back. I spoke to Dad during a hospital visit the day before we went on holiday. He told me we had to go and have a good time. I smiled at him knowing how much he loved Chloe and Jake and hugged him before I left, something I'm now so grateful for. I had kept the kids a little in the dark about their grandad's health. They knew he wasn't well, but they were both still so young at 14 and 12, I wanted to protect them from the life-snatching terminal illness my dad was fading with.

Off we went on holiday and two days into the holiday, my brother, Norman, rang me and told me Dad had died. Chris saw my face and knew the subject of my phone call. I made the decision there and then to not tell the kids, wanting them to enjoy their holiday and knowing that's what Dad would have wanted. I managed to hold it together for the rest of the holiday and appreciated the memory-making with my beautiful kids, before telling Chloe and Jake about their grandad passing when we returned home.

CHAPTER 24
FLAMES OF LOVE

Living in my flat, I continued to have the kids half of the week and when I didn't have them, I would try and go out with the lads. I had also begun dating and having a few relationships of varying seriousness. It took me a little while to get into the dating scene after such a long-term relationship with Carol.

Not only as I had to get my dating confidence back, but I had my main priority to consider, Chloe and Jake. However, once I got out onto the dating scene, it became nice to meet women and have some company and a few relationships developed with some lovely women, even if they didn't become permanent. Life was good.

One week, I saw a course advertised with the local council that interested me. It was an exercise and nutrition course, aimed at training people to go on and deliver the course in the local area such as in schools and community centres. I registered and secured a place then went along for the first session. The instructor was a lady called Gillian and I was immediately attracted to her. She was and still is a very beautiful woman, inside and out.

The course was every weekend for around four weeks and after the first session, I spent extra time grooming myself in preparation for the next session. I definitely felt there was a spark and remember she was wearing some red leggings that she looked incredible in.

As I got to know her a little (as much as you could during a training course), I really liked her personality and craic — beauty and banter, the perfect mix and I found myself trying extra hard to impress her. Towards the end of the course, details were passed around in handouts and her contact number at the council was on one of the documents.

After the training finished, I thought *fuck it*, and sent her a cheeky text saying how the course was excellent and some other bullshit then asked what the chances were of taking her out. Basically, something along the lines of the course was okay, but I'm more interested in you — "shy bairns get nowt," as we say! She sent a lovely message back saying thank you and if she wasn't with her current partner she would have thought about it. A slam of the door in my face, I was gutted but at least I'd tried.

Not long after the course, I joined a local gym and would train as much as I could with a good squad of lads. Gillian was a spin instructor at the same gym, and we would bump into each other now and then. There were definitely some eyes going on, us looking at one another along with hellos and small talk as little fireworks went off in my stomach.

Often, I would be out and about locally, perhaps in the shops or bank, and would sometimes see her. Crossing paths a lot and feeling perhaps it was serendipity. We would chat, generally, but I knew she was in a relationship, and I would be dating or in a relationship much of the time. I never stopped fancying her though, I was smitten.

One time I was at the gym and Gillian was there. Adrenaline pumping through me from my workout, I thought *fuck it* again, and decided to mention going for a drink together. I wasn't dating, after splitting with a woman I had been seeing for about nine months. She was a lovely lass, but she wasn't the one for me.

I got the impression over the last few times Gillian and I bumped into one another that perhaps she wanted me to ask her out. So I did, asking casually, whilst sweating from more than my workout. Amongst the usual general patter, I took a deep breath and asked her if she fancied meeting up one time. She answered with a yes and I almost air punched.

It had been about a year and a half of sliding doors before I got the girl. Well, I didn't quite have her yet, but the cocky little bugger in me knew I had played the long game and yeah, I had got the girl! Gillian had only recently split from her partner and the nice thing for us was that we had already begun to get to know one another, beyond the initial, visual attraction.

It was 2007 and our first date was a drink locally. I went to pick Gillian up and she was a very dark shade of fake tan. She was quite pale normally and had a coating that looked like dark varnish on fresh wood. Hand over my mouth as she got in the car, we made a joke of it, but she still looked absolutely gorgeous, just like she did the day I first set eyes on her.

Our date was to Tynemouth, around the few pubs located in the village. I saw a lot of people I knew, chatting with them and introducing Gillian. As the night progressed, I kept seeing familiar folk in most bars. Gillian turned to me, wrinkling her brow, and asked if I was a drug dealer. She thought because I knew a lot of people that I must have been a wrong 'un. After explaining I had lived in the area all my life and knew people through football, work, mates, and the close-knit community, she relaxed a little and we ended up having an amazing first date that led to many more.

We are still together today and very happy and I'm grateful every day to be loved by such a phenomenal woman who supports me, makes me laugh, and is my best friend.

We were dating for a while before Gillian met Chloe and Jake. It was during a local music gig, and she was helping the council out with stewarding the event. I was there with the kids and Julie, and her family. I spotted Gillian and beckoned her over to meet the family, who took to her instantly. It was a big deal, I didn't introduce just anyone to the kids but Gillian, well she was always streets ahead of anyone else.

Time went on at Foxtrot Green and my focus outside of work was family, exercise, and now Gillian was also a huge part of both those things. At work, jobs kept coming in, some with survivors, many, sadly with fatalities. The images of what I had seen over the years never went away, they remained, ghosts in the mind but I would use my methods to process the often-horrific sights. I became more interested in mindset and mental health, which had always been part of my life but not something I had formally studied.

Reflecting on my career, I had massively managed my own well-being and was able to process trauma by focusing my mind. It wasn't always easy, and I had developed tactics for myself that helped me in and outside of work. I wanted to learn more. The seed was planted, and it became something within me that grew. I felt the desire to help other people with their well-being through mindset and exercise and being with Gillian helped me think more about the potential.

I was based at Foxtrot Green for approximately six years in total and thoroughly enjoyed my time there, before leaving the station. I transferred to the fire station at Wallsend, Golf, in around 2011. I loved Foxtrot but by this time, Mam was living alone after Dad died. I wanted to be closer to her and available in an emergency, so I needed a quieter station as my base.

Mam, at this point, was suffering very badly from arthritis and had done for years. All of us did our bit to help but we each had commitments. Norman was in the fire service, Andrew was a mechanical engineer and worked away quite a lot, and Julie had a demanding job at the local council. So, it was important to me that I was around and at a site that felt like there was less job after job chaos, in case of an emergency with Mam.

The kids were also growing up, Chloe was 16 years old and Jake was 14 years old. Chloe had sat her GCSE exams, passing all of them; and Jake was studying at school for his exams. They were phenomenal children, and I was so proud of them, even when they were buggers — which was mainly Jake!

One time I received a call from the headmaster when Jake was in senior school. He told me he was getting suspended for bad behaviour, which the headmaster advised me involved Jake and more students running around the school causing mayhem and being boisterous. Jake came home and vehemently claimed it wasn't him, he wasn't there, and it was a case of mistaken identity. He seemed so genuine so I told him we would go to the school, and I would fight his corner. I wasn't having my bairn punished for something he hadn't done.

So off we went and on arrival at the school, I requested to see the headmaster. Going into his office, we took a seat as I prepared to assertively but politely defend my son. Explaining Jake's side of the story, I stated I disagreed with the decision and reiterated Jake's explanation that although it was his friends, he wasn't involved with the bad behaviour. The headmaster insisted Jake was there and I was having none of it, shaking my head and repeating what Jake had told me.

Then the headmaster asked me to follow him, and he subsequently took me to a room and showed me CCTV of the incident which clearly showed Jake jumping around, shouting, and playing the fool. And now I looked like an even bigger fool! Red-faced and gritting my teeth at Jake, I turned to the headmaster, apologised profusely and marched Jake out. I gave him the death stare when we left but I couldn't be angry with him for long, as to be fair, it was something I would have done, and I had to give him 10 out of 10 for being a chancer.

Work-wise, I arrived at Wallsend, Golf, on Green watch and joined another great crew. A new gaffer was coming in, Marty, and also a new proby, Graeme, who I nicknamed Dougie, after his middle name, Douglas. We all joined at the same time and gelled with the established watch. Others on the team were Peter, Rob, Leanne, Gaz, Stevie, Sticks, and Bob, with Coops, the crew manager. They had to get used to me and vice versa and I was an older man as well as an old hand. They were spot on and soon we were a blended family.

One of the larger jobs was a fire in a local haulage company, Ramage. It happened early into my time at Wallsend and again I realised I had joined a brilliant, professional watch. Golf Green had a crew that had been at the station from the start of their career. It was an excellent station but wasn't that busy, and I advised Dougie in particular to go to another station once his probation was complete, as well as suggesting to the long-term crew that they should get themselves to other stations for different experiences and learning.

Dougie was an enthusiastic proby and would always be excitedly on the lookout. One day we were all having our lunch and he came running to me to tell me there was some smoke nearby. I told him to bugger off and see the gaffer so I could eat my dinner in peace. So, he dashed over to Marty, expressing his concerns with a panic-infused voice. The gaffer reiterated we were having our dinner and it was likely someone just having a BBQ. It turned out to be a skip fire, so nothing too serious but Dougie was right.

Another time, Dougie was to complete a test allowing him to progress through his probation. The test was to be sat at the station and Dougie had been studying with the seriousness of a politician. I decided to play a trick on him and made up an exam paper including stupid questions about his watch.

One of the questions asked my preference of drink, which was always half a cup of black coffee. Another was taking the piss out of Leanne, who is a great mate and an exceptional fire fighter, but I used to mock her about her eyes. I would always mention she had a lazy eye and the question on Dougie's fake paper asked where do Leanne's tears go when she cries? The answer being down her back! Of course, it was all in jest and Leanne could give as good as she got – and her eyes were perfect.

The test time came, and Dougie went into the room with my test paper. Me, Rob, Pete, and Leanne all watched from the window, like little kids, shoulders moving with laughter as Dougie frowned, staring at the paper, and scratching his head. He started laughing, before we eventually gave him the real test. Dougie passed the genuine test, he was a brilliant firefighter and extremely intelligent. A great lad and a great laugh.

One time in Golf Green, there was a job for a house fire in Percy Main. We arrived to attend to the blaze in an upstairs flat and Leanne and I got into action. There were no people in the property so once the fire was out, we stood on the pavement and serviced our BA sets in case we received another call. As we were getting organised we saw a woman coming towards us with a pig on a lead. Now this wasn't your cute, pink, "awww" moment pig, this was a massive, black, grunting beast that was happily trotting along on a lead – you could say as happily as a pig in shit! We all started laughing and the pig owner and her pig, called Yum-Yum, came over to say hello.

Time went on at Wallsend and I was getting closer to retirement. I brought some years over from the Marines, so it meant I only had a few years left in the fire service until I could retire. I had completed a course to be a personal trainer years earlier, around the time Carol and I split up. I did it partly for my own well-being and coping mechanisms as well as to get knowledge around my life-long love of fitness. Half of the course was online, and the other half was practical, and it took around six months for me to qualify. After completing the course, it enhanced my skills and knowledge and I began to get the odd client, increasing in numbers as the years passed. It was something I thought I could develop once I retired from the fire service.

Before retirement, and after four years at Golf Green, it was time for another move, which would be by final role in Tyne and Wear Fire Service. A new area initiative was announced to amalgamate some shifts as a trial in two stations across the service, in an attempt to save money. One of these schemes was going to be trialed at Rainton Bridge, in Houghton-le-Spring.

The scheme combined two shift patterns meaning basically that you stayed at the station for four days solid before having four days off. The two stations were chosen as they were quiet areas. It also meant an enhancement in pension and a pay rise, so it felt like the perfect way to end my career in the fire service.

In July 2014, I headed over to my new station, called Hotel. I chatted with my mam, who at this point was living in extra care housing, and she told me to go for it, encouraging me just as she had all my life. I felt confident, with my siblings around and her carers, that she would be okay with me being away half of the week and it meant on my rest days, I had more time to spend with her.

Off I went, leaving my Wallsend family but knowing I'd see them in a few weeks for a pint. All of the watch who were at Golf Green went on to soar; promotions and moves to other stations. Dougie is a station manager now and is actually Chloe's boss. Amazing people and I'm proud of them all.

The watch at Station Hotel was phenomenal. Ronnie was the gaffer, who has since sadly passed away. Other teammates were Ron, Blackie, Carlos, and Keith. Then other good lads on the opposite shift including Norman and Barry. Most were Mackem's, supporting Newcastle's rival football team, Sunderland A.F.C. We had some friendly banter about the game and soon became a tight-knit team that even football couldn't divide.

It was a busier site than expected but not crazy busy and the station had all we could need: our own rooms, a gym, kitchen, and communal lounge. A home from home and I settled in, enjoying the role and the surroundings.

Our gaffer, Ronnie, was a great character. He was well known in the Birtley area as a local legend. He used to be a boxer, followed by a boxing trainer and promoter, so was a bit of a community celebrity. Ronnie had a gym in Birtley and when he was at Hotel, he would invite his boxers in to train at the station. It was great entertainment, and I got the chance to go running with the boxers and do a bit of training.

As the months passed, Ronnie's health began to deteriorate, and he told us he had been diagnosed with cancer. We looked after Ronnie just like he looked after his team — watching each other's back, offering words of encouragement, and laughs. He retired a few months before I did and sadly, subsequently passed away.

The final weeks in my role approached and eventually, it was my last shift at Tyne and Wear Fire Service in April 2016. A day that already had a lot of emotions for me before it started. Over two decades in the role, multiple fire families, and hundreds of jobs. It hadn't just been my duty; it had been my identity for so long, and a sadness travelled through my body as I put my boots on for the final time that day.

During that last shift, a job came in for us to attend a hanging in the nearby woods. Entering the area, we approached as a crew and saw a body in the distance. Blackie and Carlos turned to me and said that they would go and retrieve the body and for me to wait there. I said no, wanting to help my team but they insisted. I knew why and the care from my fellow watch overwhelmed me. Such a nice touch by my team, not wanting my final job to leave an image of the man who had taken his own life.

The next morning it was time to go. Goodbye to over 25 years in the fire service. My emotions were like a yo-yo that morning. I packed up, had a word with myself, and left my room with a heart heavier than my bags. I didn't want a big fuss and I placed all my belongings in my car as the lads clapped, big cheers and big smiles. Biting my lip, I said my goodbyes, or more like see you all soon, and I drove away.

Taking a deep breath, I turned the corner and once out of sight I pulled up — and that's when I had my moment. All those years, all those people, experiences, and learning. All the rescues, lives saved, and lives tragically lost. It was the end. The end of my era as a firefighter and time for a new chapter.

Tyne and Wear Fire Service passing out

Delta Green

Delta Green

Delta Green night out

Foxtrot Green

Foxtrot Green

Golf Green

Golf Green

Station Hotel

Station Hotel

**My last shift and Jake's first
with Tyne and Wear Fire Service**

CHAPTER 25
FRAGILITY OF HEALTH

I was 52 years old when I retired from the fire service in early 2016. By this time the kids had finished school. Chloe was 22 years old and Jake, aged 20. Chloe had left school as a confident, kind young woman. During high school, she helped out with a weekly club, supporting people with special needs and she had a natural empathy with folk.

She went on to study A-Levels, alongside a part-time job at a local toy shop. After finishing her A-Levels, she worked full-time at the toy shop until deciding to study for a business management degree whilst keeping her job on – a hard worker always striving for the next opportunity and wanting to develop her skills. She was promoted to manager at the store and was there a few years before setting up her own business as a bookkeeper. Then she also joined Tyne and Wear Fire Service part-time in the fire safety department.

When Chloe was 23 years old, she was diagnosed with MS (multiple sclerosis). The catalyst that led to medical exploration and her subsequent diagnosis happened when Chloe and me were out walking. Strolling through town, we were chatting and as she looked at me, I noticed her eyes simply weren't right. They visibly looked strange, and I asked if she was okay. Replying she was, I told her that her eyes didn't look normal, and suggested we pop into the opticians. I didn't have a clue what it was, but I knew it wasn't right and I tried to remain calm as my instinct to protect began ringing in my ears.

The opticians examined Chloe's eyes and said it wasn't her vision but recommended we visited the eye infirmary at the RVI hospital. Travelling straight up, we met Carol there and Chloe was assessed by a doctor who transpired to be an MS specialist consultant. After examination he stated that until further tests were completed, he couldn't be sure but suspected it was MS.

We listened intently but it all felt like a blur of information, and I put my hands to my head thinking this couldn't be happening to my baby. Automatically, I assumed the worst, as we tend to do with any chronic illness. Taking deep breaths, I tried to comfort Chloe as waves of fear and frustration washed over me. I wanted to protect her and right then, I couldn't.

MRI scans were conducted, and they identified lesions on Chloe's brain. As the consultant was a pioneer in the field, he mentioned there was a new trial procedure that he wanted to test out on Chloe, as she met the criteria for the best outcomes. It immediately felt like a positive option, a rope to help pull her further away from such a detrimental illness.

The treatment drug was called Alemtuzumab but is more commonly known as Lemtrada. When we were discussing treatment, Chloe was shown a range of options including the trial yearly infusion of Lemtrada. The consultant explained that many patients try other, less invasive routes first, but often without success and that many patients have to try multiple treatments before they find something that works for them, with varying degrees of success.

It sounded intense, both emotionally and physically but looking at my girl, I saw the determination in her beautiful eyes, and I knew if anyone could do it, our Chloe could. It was a decision of possibly wasting time by Chloe trying a treatment with no results, that she would be on for life. Or try this new treatment, which although slightly more invasive and intense, had a potentially much higher success rate.

Chloe, as brave as she was back when she was two years old and split her head open at the local shopping centre, opted for the Lemtrada treatment. It involved a five-day infusion, followed one year later by a three-day infusion, and then hopefully nothing again for the rest of her life.

At the time, Chloe was also in the fortunate position to be offered Lemtrada as it is rarely accessible due to expense and has only shown to be effective in patients that meet certain criteria. Her consultant mentioned Chloe's age, how early they believed they had detected her MS, and the number of relapses she had experienced which made the chances of Lemtrada working relatively high.

She was an ideal candidate, and discovered in a recent appointment that the RVI hospital has only put 200 patients through Lemtrada, which isn't a lot for a drug that has been around for almost 10 years. Chloe was really lucky and her positive, resilient attitude and outlook on life I'm sure, made the whole process easier for her.

In patients with MS, the immune system attacks the protective sheath (myelin) that covers nerve fibres, causing communication problems between the brain and the rest of the body. The way Lemtrada works is to wipe out a patient's white blood cells and in turn, immune system, with the intention they will rebuild again "forgetting" what they used to do, and therefore not attack the myelin anymore.

The more I heard about MS and the treatment, the more I felt conflicted about the severity of the illness and the hope from medical advancements. From the day both she and Jake were born, my world changed forever. They needed me, they would always need me, and it was my most important and precious duty. There's a helplessness when your child is ill, and it's magnified to unexplainable amounts when you can't do anything about it.

I felt imprisoned, unable to protect her and make things better. I remember trying to keep it together for Chloe and I turned to her, voice shaking, telling her I'd always have her back and we love her so much. She looked at me and smiled, demonstrating her life-long hard-cookie resilience, and responded with,

'Dad, it is what it is.'

She was remarkable and still is. Her strength, her mindset, her positive outlook on life. If she could bottle it and sell it, the world would be a happier place and she would be a millionaire! As soon as I heard her say that, I knew she would be okay and that she'd never give in to anything in life. My little warrior.

We got on with life until her treatment started which involved a five-day infusion of the Lemtrada drug, along with saline flushes, steroids, and antibiotics being administered. The monitoring was crucial due to the risk of the drugs, so she often had to stay in the hospital for hours after the infusion. It was gruelling but Chloe kept positive, a smile on her face even with the challenge ahead and all the associated emotions.

Once the infusion was over for the week, the medical team advised us that the next few weeks would be critical for Chloe not catching an infection as, essentially, she had no immune system. To this day, Chloe is still more susceptible to catching illnesses than your average person.

After the treatment it was hoped her immune system would build itself back up, and when almost back to normal a year later, she was scheduled to undergo the same process again, but only for three days. And that's what happened, followed by monitoring for five years past her final infusion. Thankfully, all was okay during those last five years.

Before the Lemtrada treatments, Chloe's MRI test identified numerous lesions on her brain which represented MS relapses. Following the treatment, they wanted to be able to compare MRI scans year after year and hoped to see no new lesions, which would show the treatment was working. Chloe's lesions have actually started to fade and mend themselves. She's now in a post-monitoring period, checking in with the MS nurse team yearly.

I'm certain that she managed so well because of her positive mindset, almost an extra medicine. She just got on with it, like she has with any challenges in life. Never allowing the negative to drain her. Her strength keeps me in check and if I hear myself moaning, I remember what she's gone through, with minimal complaints and maximum positivity.

She doesn't give two fucks about MS and just keeps going! She's my inspiration. She also had great support from her partner, Dylan, who she has been with for several years and is now part of the family.

As for my son, after leaving school, Jake joined an apprenticeship as a welder. He served his time locally at Smith's Docks in North Shields and worked there for around four years. He also played football in his spare time for a few of my mates, keeping fit, and enjoying one of his lifelong passions.

One of my mates mentioned Jake considering becoming a firefighter and he came home one night at 21 years old and asked if I thought he could get into the fire service. I absolutely knew he could, and he began to train for the assessment process and subsequently succeeded in securing a job as a firefighter.

He's been in the fire service for a few years now and is 27 years old, working at my old station in Byker and I couldn't be prouder. A hard worker with a selfless nature and, like his sister, always wants to be the best he can be. I admire my boy for his drive and ambition, and I'm delighted that he's followed in my footsteps. He's an incredible young man who is focused, has a heart of gold, and has his head screwed on. He has a lovely girlfriend, Ellie, who is also part of the family, and they make a beautiful couple.

After leaving Station Hotel and the Tyne and Wear Fire and Rescue Service altogether, I had a massive retirement party in Newcastle. It was magnificent to be surrounded by all the fire service families I had been part of during my time in the job. Some of us also went on a holiday to Benidorm, which was great craic and I knew that even though I wouldn't see them everyday, my fire service families were friends for life.

Despite retiring as a firefighter, I wasn't retiring altogether. Working had been part of my identity for so long, it was my daily routine, like brushing my teeth. I was by no means ready to not work, and I'm not sure if I'll ever give up work completely. On retiring from the fire service, I had a plan in mind for my personal training business. Thanks to a friend, I was able to occupy a gym space in a local rugby club where I could train clients.

I began building up my client base and enjoying the elements of having my own business and autonomy as well as doing something I thoroughly enjoyed and knew made a difference to people. In late 2016, a place became available at my current business base, not far from my home.

It felt strange being a lone ranger, working in a team of one after always being surrounded by so many colleagues. Luckily, my base is a shared building and it's nice to be around other people, even though we work for different companies. It's a great venue and I work with a variety of people as customers, some of which I have worked with from day one. In many ways, it doesn't feel like work. Physical and mental well-being is something that has always been a part of my life, meaning my business feels more like a lifestyle choice that I can enjoy and assist other people to benefit from.

Retirement from the fire service and being my own boss allowed me more time to spend with my mam, who remained in the same extra care accommodation. Her arthritis was severe, but she never complained, always so positive and grateful for us all.

At the end of 2019, the Covid-19 pandemic began to appear on the news, followed by our memorable first lockdown in March 2020. Like many businesses, I had to close, but I decided to work with people online. This included filming fitness and health related videos and posting them on Facebook for people to watch and hopefully learn from and even join in with.

I would post videos daily, and Gillian soon got involved with some of them, helping with exercise routines. We became a great team, filming fitness with a bit of banter and laughs then sharing them in the hope that they would helps others with a least a little smile and chuckle. It felt like a strange way of working for me initially, as I got my gym clothes on and moved about the house, capturing the exercises on my mobile phone — but it was equally important for my own mindset and well-being to keep working and keep fit.

As I got ready each day for work in the kitchen or lounge, I kept myself motivated knowing it could help even one person and that was enough to fuel me to keep going. The videos ended up getting thousands of views and positive feedback. People joined in and had a bit of a laugh at me trying to record and chatting to the screen before starting a workout.

It was also something for Gillian and me to do together, to keep us going at a time that was challenging for everyone in their own way. It wasn't even all about exercise for people, it was the interaction, some much-needed routine in an uncertain time, and a bit of a laugh. The joke was often on us, but the message was clear – to try and make people feel a little joy during such a traumatic time.

Mam was in the extra care home, so I knew she was okay and had a little company from the carers. Even though we couldn't visit her, being aware she wasn't alone was a big comfort. Mam was admitted into the hospital with something non-Covid related and was transferred to a respite place on hospital discharge but soon caught Covid. The accommodation was near my home, and she was placed in a room on the ground floor.

I would pass her window each day when we were all allowed a limited amount of time outside, and give her a wave and blow a kiss. She would smile and I would feel the love back from her, despite the glass and brick walls separating us. This went on until one day I passed her window and knew it was for the last time.

I looked in, ready to see my precious mam smile back and my stomach dropped. The light had gone out in her eyes, the light that had always shone brighter than any star in the sky. They were dull and she was tired. I stared at her, trying to keep the smile on my face as I swallowed the lump in my throat and felt my heart beat faster.

Mam put her thumb up to me and held my gaze. I knew it was her saying she was okay but that she'd had enough. It was her goodbye. She'd experienced years of pain with arthritis. She'd felt such heartbreak after losing Dad, her life partner, and I know in many ways she thought she was a burden to us. She never was and I would have walked the earth barefoot for her.

I got a call that night that she was being admitted to hospital and she died two days later, aged 84. I was helpless and unable to rescue her, and the cruel illness took Mam, like it snatched the lives of so many. We couldn't all see her, due to the restrictions at the time and as a piece of my soul turned black, I took massive comfort in that I had my goodbye, our moment at the window.

I also felt a little relief in knowing she would no longer be in pain after living with crippling arthritis for so long. Mam was always so strong and positive and passed her tenacity on to Chloe. Julie was the last person to see Mam alive and I'm blessed that I got to see her and say goodbye, in our own way.

All the times she had protected me, a shield around me — as a kid and as an adult. Even from afar, I knew in battle, she was there with me, her love keeping me safe and strong. The head of our family was gone and now Mam and Dad are together, and forever carried in my heart.

I decided to do a challenge in memory of Mam, and I began looking on the internet for something that would be right for me. There is a guy named David Goggins who wrote a book titled *Can't Hurt Me*. He set up a challenge called the Goggins Challenge. It involved running four miles every four hours for 48 hours, including through the night.

I decided I would do the challenge to raise money for an arthritis charity for Mam and a MS charity for Chloe. The challenge started at midnight the day after we buried Mam. I mentioned it to friends and family and shared it on social media. Jake decided to do it with me, from his home but also came and ran a few times alongside me, both of us knowing that every step was for our family and other families suffering with chronic illnesses.

Friends joined in as well, it was like *Forrest Gump*. I lived at the marina at the time and the neighbours were coming out banging pans to cheer me on and keep me motivated. It was amazing and overwhelming, and I was grateful for all the support. The local newspaper even heard about it, and I was on the front page.

The challenge helped to raise over £5,000 for the charities. It meant so much to me and even more to the charities who research and support the understanding, prevention, and treatment of chronic illnesses. People were so generous in their donations and their encouragement. Along with the funds for the chosen charities, I hope that it helped raise awareness about the conditions and perhaps even gave people ideas to fundraise themselves. It was brilliant and it helped me to process my grief and I really hope Mam was watching from somewhere.

CHAPTER 26
MINDSET AND LIFE LESSONS

After losing Mam, life had to go on albeit with a big void. Added to this loss, we had another worry as a family in late 2021, when Julie was diagnosed with breast cancer. Following a routine mammogram, some abnormalities were identified, leading to a biopsy. In early 2023, Julie was diagnosed with stage three breast cancer and subsequently received surgery in March 2023, followed by radiotherapy.

It was a frightening time, especially for Julie. However, like all of the other women in our family, Julie is brave and strong and remained positive throughout, often reassuring us at times! She was incredible and was thankfully given the all clear in April 2023.

Throughout grieving for Mam and Julie being unwell, we supported one another as a family and, as I had throughout my life, I used exercise to help me cope. Running and sessions in the gym allowed me time to process thoughts and clear my mind as well as physically making me feel better. I was living proof of my own sales pitch to my customers.

My client list for my personal training business developed and I became more aware than ever of the intricate relationship between mental and physical health. That one without the other doesn't seem to work, and that people certainly can't thrive without them working in sync. I also began reflecting more than ever on the importance of a positive mindset, especially in a world of negativity and during the time of devastation that the pandemic had brought. The distress and loss that many of us had never previously experienced in our lives and the catastrophic impact that changed the world in ways forever.

Mindset helped me with so much in life and not only me, but it had helped those close to me. During all my roles in my career, there were unwritten rules, processes, and an emphasis on mindset — part of our training that went beyond a lecture hall. Something in us that was pulled to the surface and nurtured, polished into an instinct for many.

However, it wasn't just in my career, mindset was all around me. Mam and Julie were great examples of this. Chloe, battling through her illness and always remaining positive, and Jake who entered the fire service with all the pressure that it brings – his strength of character, an absolute credit to him. All inspiring to me and others. I wanted to know more, learn more, and offer more to my clients, friends, and family.

At this time, the pandemic was still an issue and life wasn't completely back to normal but I found a specialist course online, training to become a mental health and exercise coach. It was an accredited course through a guy called Dan Hancock. It sounded right up my street and very in-depth, allowing me to have a greater understanding and the qualification that carries the reputation of knowing your stuff.

I wanted to learn more for myself as well as put it into practice in my business, aware of the interlinked relationship to overall well-being. It was an excellent course and the knowledge and information have enabled me to support people on a deeper level and understand certain issues such as managing anxiety, PTSD, eating disorders and body dysmorphia.

During the pandemic, as soon as I was allowed to open the gym, I offered free training sessions for any NHS staff and those employed in the care profession. I was inundated but I was delighted to be able to help the people who were helping the country, despite dealing with their own fears and losses. Exercise was so important as a stress release and coping mechanism, it had been a tool for me personally at countless points in my life — my own medicine.

But alongside the exercise, I started being aware of possible signs of any underlying emotional needs, and ways to talk through problems with clients. It included exploring people's anxiety and low mood, negative habits, and barriers, and looking at coping techniques via exercise and changing thought processes. Basic solution-focused work and structure that could make a positive impact.

I also established an offshore, online health and fitness academy. Since I worked away a lot during my career, I understand what it can feel like to be alone in your room, away from home and possibly struggling. Exercise and mindset can be tools to manage anxiety, low mood, build resilience, and generally give people a positive focus whilst maintaining health.

Now, thanks to my experience and training, I am able to help clients holistically. There is trust, a rapport, and in many ways, I play the role of almost a support worker at times. But I get so much from it; it keeps me well physically and mentally. Having my own business means I get a healthy work-life balance, working part-time and having time at home.

Time with Gillian, the kids, my siblings and their families. Catching up with friends, exercising and walking our dog, Teddy. We have holidays as families and make as many memories as we can. And I will keep working as long as possible, work that never really feels like work.

I'm very lucky that throughout my career, I have enjoyed all my jobs. Employment is a massive part of our lives; it shouldn't be something we loathe or that fills us with anxiety and stress. If it is, is it really worth it? My jobs have never felt easy, but they've felt right – the perfect fit for me. Well maybe not so much the brief close protection stint, but on the whole my career has been diverse, rewarding and with a great bunch of people.

We spend so much of our lives working, often more time with our work family than our own family, so the importance of being around good folk is paramount. Not always achievable and don't get me wrong, there was the odd shithead, but on the whole, my work family were like brothers (and sisters) and I'm thankful to them for making my career something that I hold fondly. Camaraderie, loyalty, support, humour, empathy, respect, and solid friendship – they all made our teams work and what more can you ask of your colleagues than that?

Life has been kind, even when challenging, I've been surrounded by a sponge of love to absorb sadness. I hope I've been able to repay the important people in my life — being there when they've needed me.

My siblings are all happy and healthy. Norman worked at Tynemouth fire station and is now retired. He's remained married to Sandra, and they have their daughter, Sally who is a manager at a local department store. I see him every few weeks for a pint or two. Andrew works away still, and we catch up when we can. He works hard and has a lovely home with his wife, Tracey, and daughter, Alex, who's just graduated from university. Then my sister, Julie, works for the local council. She has her husband, Mark and daughter, Abbie, who is also a firefighter. All amazing kids.

We are blessed, and I try to remember that daily. The definition of being happy for me is having love, family, friends, and health. It's not about money and material things, I'm sure there are many unhappy millionaires.

Every parent is proud, but my kids, they are my heartbeat and I'm thankful every day that I have them. They bring good into the world, and I would swim all the oceans to get to them if they needed me. Both of my children have done well, making themselves, their mam, and me proud. It goes beyond their achievements in school or work — they are great people. Kind, decent young adults who are polite, respectful, and thoughtful.

For as long as I can, I will continue to be a mentor with my work, to try and help, encourage and support the clients I train. I'll maintain being a mate to friends old and new and hope that they will always reach out when they want to share news, whether it be good or bad. I'll forever work on myself to be the best version of me, and I vow to keep trying to be the best dad, partner, brother, and uncle that I possibly can be. After all, it's my most important duty, and one I'm forever grateful to have.

Dad

Mam and Julie

Jake, me and Chloe

Julie and me

Jake, my brothers, Mark, and me

Chloe, me, and Jake

Skiing trip with the family

Chloe, me, and Jake

Jake, me, and Chloe

Carol's wedding

Me with Teddy

Me and Gillian

Me and Jake

Me and Chloe

Me and Gillian

Dave, me, and John

Nights out with the lads – original Delta Green

K-Company lads

Me, my brothers, and Jake

Mam and Me

Cheers!

ACKNOWLEDGEMENTS

Thank you for reading DUTY. I hope you enjoyed reading it as I relived my life — perhaps laughing at times, with me and at me! I also hope it resonated with you and even made you think about where your own duty lies in life. I needed to get my story out into the world because, in many ways, we are all the same: responsibilities we have, the path we walk, the family and friendships we treasure, our love and losses, and things that get us through it all, the good and the bad. Each of us has a story.

My story couldn't have been told without the support from my publisher, Write on the Tyne Publishing, so thank you to the team for making DUTY more than just a story in my head. And of course, my story is my story due to the many incredible people I have met in my life and who have influenced my journey — I thank you all.

My mam, Harriet. You were quite simply an inspiration to all of us. Your courage, strength, and kindness even going through your own adversity, was a constant reminder to me to be the best person I could be. You have been by my side, and in my thoughts all along the way. Your duty as a mother and grandmother was unwavering. I'm proud to be your son — I love you and miss you so much.

Dad, I know you struggled to show it sometimes, but we all knew that you loved us and worked hard to provide for us. You taught us so much and we will always be thankful. The times you shared with your grandkids were precious and will stay with them and me forever.

Chloe and Jake, I am so proud of you both from being kids to the amazing, caring, thoughtful adults you have become. You've never let me or yourselves down, and I will try to never let you down. Keep believing in yourself as much as I do. I will always have your back, no matter what life throws at you. Never, ever forget how much I love you.

My Gillian, thank you for being my constant support and for making our life together an amazing journey. You are the kindest, most caring and most thoughtful person in the world. You mean everything to me and you make me a better person. I look forward to the future with you — filled with fun, adventure, and many memories. I love you, always.

My family; Norm, Andrew, and Julie, thank you for being the best brothers and sister I could ever wish for. We have always been there for each other and always will be. Thank you to Mark, Sandra, and Tracey for being a huge part of our family, and thank you to my three beautiful nieces, Sally, Abbie, and Alex.

Thank you to all my work families across my career. To the men of 160 troop — we all joined as raw recruits in 1981, we embarked on one of the longest and toughest military training courses in the world. The sheer hardship, adversity, and uncompromising challenges we endured together to become Royal Marines will stay with me forever. Respect and thanks to you all.

K-Company, 42 Commando, Royal Marines — when I joined this great fighting unit none of us knew what lay ahead. As we were all called to duty, to serve our country in war, we could never have imagined the battles we would go through together as young men. But we prevailed, through guts, determination, and sheer endeavour. We are part of the history of the Royal Marines and this great country. The friendship and camaraderie we forged will never pass. I am proud to have served with you all. RIP to all those who are no longer with us.

Special thanks to Jock McKenzie, Richard Everritt, Kevin Dale and Leon Barker for your input in the early days.

My fire service family — my career in the fire service took me on a journey from recruits course to still being operational when I retired in 2016. The friendships and bonds I made are still with me now. From my training course to Delta Green, Foxtrot Green, Golf Green, and then Station Hotel, I have had the enormous pleasure of working alongside some of the best professional, dedicated people I know. We have been through some horrendous and challenging experiences together along with funny and unbelievable events. I will cherish the memories and laughter we shared forever. My heartfelt thanks to you all.

If you enjoyed reading DUTY, please leave a review on Amazon and Goodreads. Reviews help make books visible to other people and leaving a review is the best way to thank an author and the team behind an author for the hours and hours it takes to produce a book. If you would like to know more about me and more about Write on the Tyne, visit www.writeonthetyne.com.